IMMORTAL FIRE

GREEK, PERSIAN AND MACEDONIAN WARS

Written by Richard Bodley Scott, assisted
by Nik Gaukroger, James Hamilton
and Paul Robinson

OSPREY
PUBLISHING

SLITHERINE

First published in Great Britain in 2008 by Osprey Publishing Ltd.

Osprey Publishing, Midland House, West Way, Botley, Oxford OX2 0PH, UK
443 Park Avenue South, New York, NY 10016, USA
E-mail: info@ospreypublishing.com

Slitherine Software UK Ltd., The White Cottage, 8 West Hill Avenue, Epsom, KT 19 8LE, UK
E-mail: info@slitherine.co.uk

A CIP catalogue record for this book is available from the British Library

ISBN: 978 1 84603 346 9

Rules system written by Richard Bodley Scott, Simon Hall, and Terry Shaw
Page layout by Myriam Bell
Index by Glyn Sutcliffe
Typeset in Joanna Pro and Sleepy Hollow
Cover artwork by Peter Dennis
Photography by Duncan MacFarlane – Wargames Illustrated
Page design features supplied by istockphoto.com
All artwork and cartography © Osprey Publishing Ltd
Project management by JD McNeil & Simone Drinkwater
Technical management by Iain McNeil
Originated by PDQ Media, UK
Printed in China through Worldprint Ltd

08 09 10 11 12   10 9 8 7 6 5 4 3 2 1

FOR A CATALOGUE OF ALL BOOKS PUBLISHED BY OSPREY MILITARY AND AVIATION
PLEASE CONTACT:

NORTH AMERICA
Osprey Direct, c/o Random House Distribution Center, 400 Hahn Road,
Westminster, MD 21157
E-mail: info@ospreydirect.com

ALL OTHER REGIONS
Osprey Direct UK, P.O. Box 140 Wellingborough, Northants, NN8 2FA, UK
E-mail: info@ospreydirect.co.uk

FOR DETAILS OF ALL GAMES PUBLISHED BY SLITHERINE SOFTWARE UK LTD e-mail
info@slitherine.co.uk

Osprey Publishing is supporting the Woodland Trust, the UK's leading woodland conservation charity, by funding the dedication of trees.

www.ospreypublishing.com

www.slitherine.com

CONTENTS

INTRODUCTION

Field of Glory is a historical miniature tabletop wargaming rules system for anyone interested in recreating the battles of the ancient and medieval eras. This companion is designed to be used alongside the *Field of Glory* rulebook and covers the armies of the Classical and Hellenistic eras from the development of the hoplite system in Greece in the 7th century BC until the Hellenistic successor kingdoms that derived from the break-up of Alexander the Great's empire came into conflict with Rome from the 3rd century BC onwards.

It includes all the armies of the wars between the Greek city states and against the might of the Achaemenid Persian Empire, the Greek counter-offensive against Persia under the Macedonian King Alexander the Great, and the wars of Alexander's successors. It also details many other armies peripheral to these conflicts.

This is a period of great variety, with many different, colourful troop types vying for tactical dominance. Each army had its own special character, making this one of the most fascinating periods of military history for the wargamer to explore.

As you look at each army, you will find the following sections:

- **Brief historical notes** on the army, its wars, its famous generals, weapons and/or troop types.
- A ready-to-play **starter army** – just put it together and play a balanced small game.
- Instructions for building a **customised army** using our points system.
- A table with the full list of **compulsory** and **optional** troops.
- Supporting illustrations to give you a flavour of the period.
- Miniatures photographs.

CLASSICAL GREEK

This list covers Greek armies from the early 7th century BC until the hoplite system was replaced in Greece circa 279 BC, and until the suppression of the minor Italiot or Siciliot states in the later 3rd century BC. Syracuse has its own list from 410.

HOPLITES

The armies of Classical Greece were based on the hoplite, a type of heavy infantryman armed with spear and large shield, who fought in a solid phalanx formation, usually around eight ranks deep. The spear (doru) was approximately 2.7 metres in length and mostly used overarm. The shield (aspis) was about 1 metre in diameter. In addition to the shield, defensive equipment included body armour (thorakes), bronze helmet and greaves (shin armour).

Hoplites were a citizen militia and supplied their own equipment. Until the late 6th century BC, the majority of hoplites wore metal thorakes. In the early 5th century, the proportion with such protection dropped because the average wealth of hoplites decreased.

Greek Hoplite

Hoplites were more than a match for the Persian infantry. Following the defeat of Xerxes's invasion of Greece, the Persians themselves began to replace their line infantry with mercenary Greek hoplites. It has also been said they developed native Persian hoplites. In the early 4th century, Iphikrates experimented with a new type of equipment – linen armour, a new style of boots, a small shield (pelta) and a longer spear than the usual hoplite spear.

Later in the century, King Philip II of Macedon (father of Alexander the Great) developed the pike phalanx **(see p.43)**. This rendered the hoplite obsolete, although it took some time for the hoplite fighting style to die out, particularly in the Italian and Sicilian colonies.

Greek Cavalry

Athenian infantryman and cavalryman fighting an Euboean hoplite at the battle of Tamynae, 349 BC, by Angus McBride. Taken from Elite 7: Ancient Greeks.

PERSIAN WARS GREEK STARTER ARMY

Spartan Commander-in-Chief	1	Troop Commander (King Pausanias)
Spartan citizen hoplites	1 BG	6 bases of hoplites: Superior, Armoured, Drilled Heavy Foot – Offensive Spearmen
Spartan perioikoi hoplites	2 BGs	Each comprising 6 bases of hoplites: Average, Armoured, Drilled Heavy Foot – Offensive Spearmen
Spartan javelinmen	1 BG	8 bases of javelinmen: Poor, Unprotected, Undrilled Light Foot – Javelins, Light Spear
Corinthian allied commander	1	Troop Commander
Corinthian hoplites	2 BGs	Each comprising 6 bases of hoplites: Average, Armoured, Undrilled Heavy Foot – Offensive Spearmen
Corinthian javelinmen	1 BG	8 bases of javelinmen: Poor, Unprotected, Undrilled Light Foot – Javelins, Light Spear
Athenian allied commander	1	Troop Commander
Athenian hoplites	2 BGs	Each comprising 8 bases of hoplites: Average, Armoured, Undrilled Heavy Foot – Offensive Spearmen
Athenian archers	1 BG	6 bases of archers: Average, Unprotected, Undrilled Light Foot – Bow
Camp	1	Unfortified camp
Total	10 BGs	Camp, 68 foot bases, 3 commanders

PELOPONNESIAN WARS SPARTAN STARTER ARMY

Commander-in-Chief	1	Field Commander
Sub-commanders	2	2 x Troop Commander
Cavalry	1 BG	4 bases of cavalry: Average, Armoured, Drilled Cavalry – Light Spear, Swordsmen
Spartan citizens	2 BGs	Each comprising 8 bases of hoplites: Superior, Protected, Drilled Heavy Foot – Offensive Spearmen
Spartan perioikoi	3 BGs	Each comprising 8 bases of hoplites: Average, Protected, Drilled Heavy Foot – Offensive Spearmen
Peltasts	2 BGs	Each comprising 6 bases of peltasts: Average, Unprotected, Drilled Light Foot – Javelins, Light Spear
Slingers	1 BG	6 bases of slingers: Average, Unprotected, Undrilled Light Foot – Sling
Camp	1	Unfortified camp
Total	9 BGs	Camp, 4 mounted bases, 58 foot bases, 3 commanders

BUILDING A CUSTOMISED LIST USING OUR ARMY POINTS

Choose an army based on the maxima and minima in the list below. The following special instructions apply to this army:

- Commanders should be depicted as cavalry or hoplites.

- Minima marked * apply only if the C-in-C is of that origin.

- Unless the C-in-C is of the same origin, troops only permitted to a certain origin can only be fielded under the command of an allied general of that origin.

- An allied general's contingent must conform to the Classical Greek allies list

below, but the troops in the contingent are deducted from the minima and maxima in the main list.

Greek Javelinmen

- The minimum number of hoplite bases is reduced to 12 if the C-in-C is Aitolian, Akarnanian or Phokian, 16 if Thessalian.

Spartans at the battle of Thermopylae, 480 BC, by Richard Hook. Taken from Elite 66: The Spartan Army.

CLASSICAL GREEK

Territory Types: Agricultural, Developed, Hilly, Mountains

C-in-C	Inspired Commander/Field Commander/Troop Commander	80/50/35	1	
Sub-commanders	Field Commander/Troop Commander	50/35	0–2	
Greek allied commanders	Field Commander/Troop Commander	40/25	0–3	

Troop name		Troop Type				Capabilities		Points per base	Bases per BG	Total bases
		Type	Armour	Quality	Training	Shooting	Close Combat			
Core Troops										
Cavalry	Thessalians before 450	Light Horse	Unprotected	Average	Undrilled	Javelins	Light Spear	7	4–6	4–12
	Non–Thessalians before 450	Cavalry	Protected	Average	Undrilled	–	Light Spear	7	4–6	0–6
			Armoured					10		
	Thessalians from 450	Light Horse	Unprotected	Average	Undrilled or Drilled	Javelins	Light Spear	7	4–6	0–12 / 8–18
		Cavalry	Armoured	Superior	Undrilled	–	Light Spear, Swordsmen	16	4–6	0–8
				Superior	Drilled			17		
				Average	Undrilled			12		
				Average	Drilled			13		
	Non–Thessalians from 450	Cavalry	Armoured	Average	Undrilled	–	Light Spear	10	4–6	0–12
					Drilled			11		
		Cavalry	Armoured	Average	Undrilled	–	Light Spear, Swordsmen	12	4–6	0–12 / 4–12
					Drilled			13		
		Light Horse	Unprotected	Average	Undrilled or Drilled	Javelins	Light Spear	7	4–6	0–6
Hoplites	Only before 460	Heavy Foot	Armoured	Average	Undrilled	–	Offensive Spearmen	9	6–8	24–160
	Only from 490	Heavy Foot	Protected	Average	Undrilled	–	Offensive Spearmen	7	6–8	
Upgrade non–Spartan elite hoplites to:	Only before 460	Heavy Foot	Armoured	Superior	Drilled	–	Offensive Spearmen	13	6–8	0–8
	Only from 490	Heavy Foot	Protected	Superior	Drilled	–	Offensive Spearmen	10	6–8	
Upgrades Spartan citizens to:	Only before 460	Heavy Foot	Armoured	Superior	Drilled	–	Offensive Spearmen	13	6–8	*6–36
	Only from 490	Heavy Foot	Protected	Superior	Drilled	–	Offensive Spearmen	10	6–8	
Upgrade Spartan perioikoi to:	Only before 460	Heavy Foot	Armoured	Average	Drilled	–	Offensive Spearmen	10	6–8	*12–60
	Only from 490	Heavy Foot	Protected	Average	Drilled	–	Offensive Spearmen	8	6–8	
Downgrade Asiatic Greek, Italiot or Siciliot citizen hoplites to:	Only before 460	Heavy Foot	Armoured	Poor	Undrilled	–	Offensive Spearmen	7	6–8	Any
	Only from 490	Heavy Foot	Protected	Poor	Undrilled	–	Offensive Spearmen	5	6–8	
Upgrade hoplites to:	Only from 450 (mercenaries) / Only from 370 (citizens)	Heavy Foot	Protected	Average	Drilled	–	Offensive Spearmen	8	6–8	0–48
Javelinmen	Only Aitolians, Akarnanians, Phokians or Thessalians	Light Foot	Unprotected	Average	Undrilled	Javelins	Light Spear	4	6–8	*24–180
	Others	Light Foot	Unprotected	Poor	Undrilled	Javelins	Light Spear	2	6–8	
Peltasts	Any state, only from 450	Light Foot	Unprotected	Average	Drilled	Javelins	Light Spear	4	6–8	0–18

Optional Troops											
Cretan archers	Only from 450	Light Foot	Unprotected	Superior	Drilled	Bow	—	6	6–8	0–8	
Other archers		Light Foot	Unprotected	Average	Undrilled or Drilled	Bow	—	5	6–8	0–12	0–18
Slingers		Light Foot	Unprotected	Average	Undrilled	Sling	—	4	6–8	0–12	
Helots	Only Spartans before 450	Mob	Unprotected	Poor	Undrilled	—	—	2	8–12	0–24	
Thracians (or Agesilaus's Paphlagonian foot)		Medium Foot	Protected	Average	Undrilled	—	Light Spear	5	6–8		
Thracians	Any date	Medium Foot	Protected	Average	Undrilled	—	Offensive Spearmen	7	6–8	0–8	
	Only before 300	Medium Foot	Protected	Average	Undrilled	—	Light Spear, Swordsmen	6	6–8		
	Only from 350	Medium Foot	Protected	Average	Undrilled	—	Heavy weapon	7	6–8		
Iphikratean hoplites	Only from 380	Medium Foot	Protected	Average	Drilled	—	Offensive spearmen	8	6–8	0–8	
Stone-throwers	Only Phokians from 380	Heavy Artillery	—	Average	Drilled	Heavy Artillery	—	20	2	0–6	
Special Campaigns											
Only Spartans from 369 to 368											
Syracusan-supplied Spanish foot		Medium Foot	Protected	Average	Undrilled	—	Impact Foot, Swordsmen	7	4–8	4–8	
Syracusan-supplied Gallic foot		Heavy Foot	Protected	Average	Undrilled	—	Impact Foot, Swordsmen	7	4–8	4–8	

Spartan hoplites fight the Thebans at the battle of Koroneia, 394 BC, by Adam Hook. Taken from Warrior 27: Greek Hoplite 480–323 BC.

CLASSICAL GREEK ALLIES

Allied commander		Field Commander/Troop Commander				40/25		1	
Troop name		**Troop Type**				**Capabilities**		**Points per base**	**Bases per BG**	**Total bases**
		Type	Armour	Quality	Training	Shooting	Close Combat			
Cavalry	Thessalians before 450	Light Horse	Unprotected	Average	Undrilled	Javelins	Light Spear	7	4	0–4
	Non–Thessalians before 450	Cavalry	Protected	Average	Undrilled	–	Light Spear	7	4	0–4
			Armoured					10		
	Thessalians from 450	Light Horse	Unprotected	Average	Undrilled or Drilled	Javelins	Light Spear	7	4–6	0–6
		Cavalry	Armoured	Superior	Undrilled	–	Light Spear, Swordsmen	16	4	
				Superior	Drilled			17		
				Average	Undrilled			12		
				Average	Drilled			13		
	Non–Thessalians from 450	Cavalry	Armoured	Average	Undrilled	–	Light Spear	10	4	0–4
					Drilled			11		
		Cavalry	Armoured	Average	Undrilled	–	Light Spear, Swordsmen	12	4	
					Drilled			13		
		Light Horse	Unprotected	Average	Undrilled or Drilled	Javelins	Light Spear	7	4	
Hoplites	Only before 460	Heavy Foot	Armoured	Average	Undrilled	–	Offensive Spearmen	9	6–8	6–24
	Only from 490	Heavy Foot	Protected	Average	Undrilled	–	Offensive Spearmen	7	6–8	
Upgrades Spartan citizens to:	Only before 460	Heavy Foot	Armoured	Superior	Drilled	–	Offensive Spearmen	13	6–8	*6–12
	Only from 490	Heavy Foot	Protected	Superior	Drilled	–	Offensive Spearmen	10	6–8	
Upgrade Spartan perioikoi to:	Only before 460	Heavy Foot	Armoured	Average	Drilled	–	Offensive Spearmen	10	6–8	*6–12
	Only from 490	Heavy Foot	Protected	Average	Drilled	–	Offensive Spearmen	8	6–8	
Downgrade Asiatic Greek, Italiot or Siciliot citizen hoplites to:	Only before 460	Heavy Foot	Armoured	Poor	Undrilled	–	Offensive Spearmen	7	6–8	Any
	Only from 490	Heavy Foot	Protected	Poor	Undrilled	–	Offensive Spearmen	5	6–8	
Upgrade hoplites to:	Only from 450 (mercenaries)	Heavy Foot	Protected	Average	Drilled	–	Offensive Spearmen	8	6–8	0–18
	Only from 370 (citizens)									
Javelinmen	Only Aitolians, Akarnanians, Phokians or Thessalians	Light Foot	Unprotected	Average	Undrilled	Javelins	Light Spear	4	6–8	*6–24
	Others	Light Foot	Unprotected	Poor	Undrilled	Javelins	Light Spear	2	6–8	
Peltasts	Any state, only from 450	Light Foot	Unprotected	Average	Drilled	Javelins	Light Spear	4	6–8	0–6

*The Upgrades Spartan / perioikoi group shares an overall total of *12–18.

EARLY ACHAEMENID PERSIAN

The Achaemenid Empire (known in Old Persian as Hakhāmanishiyan) was founded by the Persian King Cyrus II the Great, who conquered the Median (550 BC), Lydian (546 BC) and Babylonian (539 BC) empires. His son Cambyses II conquered Egypt. The Persian Empire, the largest yet known in the world, then stretched from India to Egypt and the borders of Greece. In response to the mainland Greeks sending aid to rebellious Greek cities in Asia Minor, King Darius I sent a punitive expedition that was defeated at the battle of Marathon. His son, Xerxes I, sent a full scale invasion of Greece that was also defeated – the decisive battles being at Salamis by sea and Plataea by land. Thereafter the Persian kings contented themselves with using their vast wealth to subsidise various Greek city states in turn, and hence encourage the Greeks (if any encouragement was needed) to fight amongst themselves and prevent any one state from achieving dominance. This policy was successful until the second half of the 4th century BC, when the previously backward kingdom of Macedon, under the rule of Philip II, achieved control over the whole of Greece, and turned its eyes eastwards. Philip's son Alexander the Great invaded the Persian Empire in 334 BC and rapidly conquered it (**see p.41**).

This list covers Achaemenid Persian armies from 550 BC, when Cyrus the Great defeated the Medes, until 420 BC.

The Achaemenid Empire © Osprey Publishing Ltd. Taken from Shadows in the Desert: Ancient Persia at War.

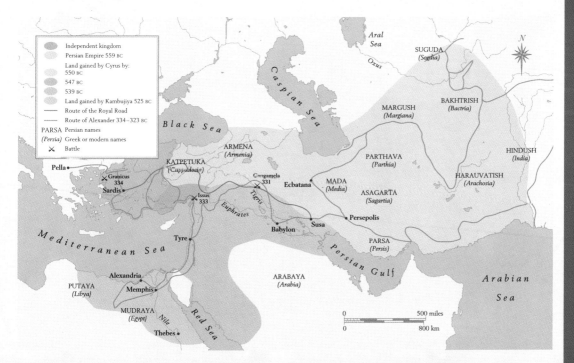

TROOP NOTES

Persian and Median cavalry are described by Herodotus as armed the same as their foot. This has previously been taken as meaning that they were armed with bow and spear. However, the majority of contemporary illustrations show them wielding bows. Recently discovered Achaemenid tomb paintings showing scenes of Darius I's campaign against the Skythians depict mounted Achaemenid and Skythian archers charging into each other while shooting. All are armed with sagaris (long-handled axes) and none carry spears. We therefore classify them as Bow, Swordsmen.

The Immortals and the Persian, Median, Hyrkanian, Kissian and Persian Gulf Exile foot formed up behind a barrier of large wicker shields. It appears that the Immortals were all equipped with short spear as well as bow, but only the first few ranks of the others had spears. None were capable of matching a Greek hoplite spear phalanx, so we classify their close combat weaponry as Light Spear. The later archers and spearmen equipped with crescent-shaped shields can be deployed separately or in mixed battle groups.

There is also evidence for the mustering of bow-armed chariotry with 3 or 4 crew during Darius I's reign.

Immortal

Persian Immortals, c. 333 BC, by Simon Chew. Taken from Elite 42: The Persian Army 550–330 BC.

The Greek and Persian Wars 492 – 480 BC © Osprey Publishing Ltd. Taken from Shadows in the Desert: Ancient Persia at War.

EARLY ACHAEMENID PERSIAN STARTER ARMY		
Commander-in-Chief	1	Field Commander (Mardonius)
Sub-commanders	2	2 x Troop Commander
Persian and Median cavalry	2 BGs	Each comprising 4 bases of Persian and Median cavalry: Superior, Armoured, Undrilled Cavalry – Bow, Swordsmen
Saka cavalry	1 BG	4 bases of Saka cavalry: Average, Unprotected, Undrilled Light Horse – Bow, Swordsmen
Immortals	1 BG	8 bases of Immortals: Superior, Armoured, Drilled Medium Foot – Bow, Light Spear
Persian and Median foot	2 BGs	Each comprising 6 bases of Persian and Median foot: Average, Protected, Undrilled Medium Foot – half Bow, Light Spear, half Bow
Bactrian and Saka foot	1 BG	6 bases of Bactrian and Saka foot: Poor, Unprotected, Undrilled Medium Foot – half Bow, Light Spear, half Bow
Boiotian hoplites	2 BGs	Each comprising 6 bases of hoplites: Average, Armoured, Undrilled Heavy Foot – Offensive Spearmen
Camp	1	Unfortified camp
Total	9 BGs	Camp, 12 mounted bases, 38 foot bases, 3 commanders

BUILDING A CUSTOMISED LIST USING OUR ARMY POINTS

Choose an army based on the maxima and minima in the list below. The following special instructions apply to this army:

- The C-in-C should be depicted as guard cavalry or a light chariot.

- Other commanders should be depicted as guard cavalry.
- The minimum marked * applies if any Medizing Greek troops are used.

Persian Cavalry

Persian cavalry, by Jack Cassin-Scott. Taken from Men-at-Arms 69:
The Greek and Persian Wars 500–323 BC.

EARLY ACHAEMENID PERSIAN

Territory Types: Agricultural, Developed, Hilly

C-in-C		Inspired Commander/Field Commander/Troop Commander					80/50/35		1	
Sub-commanders		Field Commander					50		0–2	
		Troop Commander					35		0–3	

Troop name		Troop Type				Capabilities		Points per base	Bases per BG	Total bases
		Type	Armour	Quality	Training	Shooting	Close Combat			
Core Troops										
Guard cavalry		Cavalry	Armoured	Elite	Drilled	Bow	Swordsmen	22	2–4	0–4
				Superior				19		
Persian or Median cavalry		Cavalry	Armoured	Superior	Undrilled	Bow	Swordsmen	18	4–6	6–12
Immortals		Medium Foot	Armoured	Superior	Drilled	Bow	Light Spear	12	6–8	0–16
			Protected					9		
Other Persian, Median, Hyrkanian, Kissian, or Persian Gulf Exile foot		Medium Foot	Protected	Average	Undrilled	Bow	Light Spear	6	1/2	6–8	0–48	12–48
		Medium Foot	Protected	Average	Undrilled	Bow	–	6	1/2		
Crescent shield archers	Only from 465	Light Foot	Unprotected	Average	Undrilled	Bow	–	5	6–8	0–24
		Medium Foot	Protected	Average	Undrilled	Bow	–	6	6–8 / 1/2 6–8	
Crescent shield spearmen	Only from 450	Medium Foot	Protected	Average	Undrilled	–	Light Spear	5	1/2 / 6–8	0–12
Optional Troops										
Achaemenid chariots	Only before 484	Heavy Chariots	–	Superior	Undrilled	Bow	–	20	4	0–4
Saka cavalry	Only from 545	Light Horse or Cavalry	Unprotected	Average	Undrilled	Bow	Swordsmen	10	4–6	0–6	0–12
Bactrian cavalry	Only from 545	Light Horse	Unprotected	Average	Undrilled	Bow	Light Spear	9	4–6	0–6
Other light horse archers		Light Horse	Unprotected	Average	Undrilled	Bow	–	8	4–6	0–6
Bactrian, Saka or similar foot		Medium Foot	Unprotected	Average	Undrilled	Bow	Light Spear	5	1/2	6–8	0–8
						Bow	–	5	1/2	
		Medium Foot	Unprotected	Poor	Undrilled	Bow	Light Spear	3	1/2	6–8	
						Bow	–	3	1/2	
Kaspian or similar archers		Light foot	Unprotected	Average	Undrilled	Bow	–	5	6–8	0–8
				Poor				3		
Armenian, Paphlagonian, Thracian or similar javelinmen		Medium Foot	Protected	Average	Undrilled	–	Light Spear	5	6–8	0–8
				Poor				3		
Mysian, Libyan, Pisidian or similar javelinmen		Light Foot	Unprotected	Average	Undrilled	Javelins	Light Spear	4	6–8	0–8
				Poor				2		
Lydian or Asiatic Greek hoplites	Only from 545 to 461	Heavy Foot	Armoured	Average	Undrilled	–	Offensive spearmen	9	4–6	0–6
				Poor				7		
	Only from 490	Heavy Foot	Protected	Average	Undrilled	–	Offensive spearmen	7	4–6	
				Poor				5		
Assyrian and Chaldaean foot		Heavy Foot	Protected	Average	Drilled	–	Light Spear, Swordsmen	7	1/2	4–6	0–6
		Medium Foot	Protected	Average	Drilled	Bow	–	7	1/2	
		Heavy Foot	Protected	Poor	Drilled	–	Light Spear, Swordsmen	5	1/2	4–6	
		Medium Foot	Protected	Poor	Drilled	Bow	–	5	1/2	
Arab camelry		Camelry	Unprotected	Poor	Undrilled	Bow	–	8	4	0–4

Troop	Availability	Type	Protection	Quality	Drill	Shoot	Weapon	Points	Bases	Count
Lykian or Phoenician marines	Only from 545	Medium Foot	Protected	Average	Undrilled	–	Light Spear, Swordsmen	6	4	0–4
				Poor				4		
Egyptian marines	Only from 525	Medium Foot	Protected	Average	Drilled	–	Defensive Spearmen	7	4	0–4
				Poor				5		
Indian foot	Only from 525	Medium Foot	Unprotected	Average	Undrilled	Bow	Swordsmen	6	4	0–4
				Poor				4		
Indian chariots	Only from 525	Heavy Chariots	–	Average	Undrilled	Bow	–	16	2	0–2
Libyan chariots	Only from 525	Light Chariots	–	Average	Undrilled	–	Light Spear	11	2	
Fortified camp								24		0–1
Allies										
Mede rebel allies (Only in 550) – See "Empires of Ancient Mesopotamia"										
Saka allies (Only in 530)										
Special Campaigns										
Only in Cyrus in Lydia in 546										
Improvised camelry	Camelry	Protected	Poor	Undrilled	Bow	Swordsmen		11	4–6	4–6
Scythed chariots	Scythed Chariots	–	Average	Undrilled	–	–		15	2–4	0–4
Moveable towers	Battle Wagons	–	Average	Undrilled	Bow	–		17	2	0–4
Only in 479										
Medizing Greek hoplites	Heavy Foot	Armoured	Average	Undrilled	–	Offensive spearmen		9	6–8	*8–16
		Protected						7		
Medizing Greek cavalry	Cavalry	Protected	Average	Undrilled	–	Light Spear		7	4	0–4
		Armoured						10		
	Light Horse	Unprotected	Average	Undrilled	Javelins	Light Spear		7		
Medizing Greek javelinmen	Light Foot	Unprotected	Poor	Undrilled	Javelins	Light Spear		2	4–6	0–6

THRACIAN

This list covers Thracian armies from the 7th century BC until 46 AD when Thrace was incorporated as a Roman province. Thrace was a Roman client kingdom from 25 BC.

TROOP NOTES

Most Thracians were armed primarily with javelins. Some, however, prior to the mid-3rd century BC at the latest, were armed with long thrusting spears. A few highly regarded mercenary units prior to the 3rd century BC were termed "swordsmen" and were probably armed with a type of forward curving one edged sword (perhaps similar to the Lykian drepanon) as well as javelins. The most famous Thracian weapon was the rhomphaia, a vicious weapon with a forward curving blade on a long handle. This may have come into use in the later 4th century BC or perhaps somewhat later. No-one is entirely sure.

THRACIAN

THRACIAN STARTER ARMY			
Commander-in-Chief	1		Field Commander
Sub-commanders	2		2 x Troop Commander
Armoured cavalry	2 BGs		Each comprising 4 bases of armoured cavalry: Superior, Armoured, Undrilled Cavalry – Light Spear, Swordsmen
Light cavalry	2 BGs		Each comprising 4 bases of light cavalry: Average, Unprotected, Undrilled Light Horse – Javelins, Light Spear
Foot with rhomphaia	4 BGs		Each comprising 8 bases of foot with rhomphaia: Average, Protected, Undrilled Medium Foot – Heavy Weapon
Skirmishers with javelins	2 BGs		Each comprising 6 bases of javelinmen: Average, Unprotected, Undrilled Light Foot – Javelins, Light Spear
Skirmishers with slings	1 BG		6 bases of slingers: Average, Unprotected, Undrilled Light Foot – Sling
Camp	1		Unfortified camp
Total	11 BGs		Camp, 16 mounted bases, 50 foot bases, 3 commanders

Thracian slinger and infantry after the battle of Kallinikos, 171 BC, by Angus McBride. Taken from Men-at-Arms 360: The Thracians 700 BC–AD 46.

BUILDING A CUSTOMISED LIST USING OUR ARMY POINTS

Choose an army based on the maxima and minima in the list below. The following special instructions apply to this army:

- Commanders should be depicted as armoured cavalry.
- The Getae cannot have allies or drilled troops.

Thracian Javelinman

THRACIAN									
Territory Types: Agricultural, Hilly, Woodlands									
C-in-C	Inspired Commander/Field Commander/Troop Commander						80/50/35		1
Sub-commanders	Field Commander						50		0–2
	Troop Commander						35		0–3
Troop name		**Troop Type**				**Capabilities**		**Points per base**	**Bases per BG**	**Total bases**
		Type	Armour	Quality	Training	Shooting	Close Combat			
Core Troops										
Armoured cavalry		Cavalry	Armoured	Superior	Undrilled	–	Light Spear, Swordsmen	16	4–6	0–8
Light horse	Getae	Light Horse	Unprotected	Average	Undrilled	Bow	–	8	4–6	10–32	8–32
	Others	Light Horse	Unprotected	Average	Undrilled	Javelins	Light Spear	7	4–6	8–32
		Light Horse	Unprotected	Average	Undrilled	Bow	–	8	4–6	0–12
Foot with javelins		Medium Foot	Protected	Average	Undrilled	–	Light Spear	5	6–8	0–160	24–160
Foot with thrusting spear	Only before 250 BC	Medium Foot	Protected	Average	Undrilled	–	Offensive Spearmen	7	6–8	0–48
"Swordsmen"	Only before 300 BC	Medium Foot	Protected	Average	Undrilled	–	Light Spear, Swordsmen	6	6–8	0–24
Foot with rhomphaia	From 350 to 251 BC	Medium Foot	Protected	Average	Undrilled	–	Heavy weapon	7	6–8	0–116
	From 250 BC									
Skirmishers with javelins		Light Foot	Unprotected	Average	Undrilled	Javelins	Light Spear	4	6–8	6–24	6–18
Skirmishers with bow		Light Foot	Unprotected	Average	Undrilled	Bow	–	5	6–8	0–12
Skirmishers with sling		Light Foot	Unprotected	Average	Undrilled	Sling	–	4	6–8	0–12
Optional Troops										
Families and slaves		Mob	Unprotected	Poor	Undrilled	–	–	2	6–8	0–8
Fortified camp								24		0–1
Allies										
Greek (mercenary) allies (Only from 400 BC to 357 BC) – Classical Greek										
Special Campaigns										
Only Roman client kingdom from 25 BC to 46 BC										
Upgrade armoured cavalry to		Cavalry	Armoured	Superior	Drilled	–	Light Spear, Swordsmen	17	4–6	0–8
Upgrade foot with javelins to		Medium or Heavy Foot	Protected	Average	Drilled	–	Light Spear, Swordsmen	7	4–8	0–24
			Armoured					9		
Roman allies – Principate Roman – See Field of Glory Companion 5: *Legions Triumphant: Imperial Rome at War*										

THRACIAN ALLIES

Allied commander	Field Commander/Troop Commander						40/25		1	
Troop name	Troop Type				Capabilities		Points per base	Bases per BG	Total bases	
	Type	Armour	Quality	Training	Shooting	Close Combat				
Armoured cavalry	Cavalry	Armoured	Superior	Undrilled	–	Light Spear, Swordsmen	16	4	0–4	
Light horse — Getae	Light Horse	Unprotected	Average	Undrilled	Bow	–	8	4–6	4–12	4–12
Light horse — Others	Light Horse	Unprotected	Average	Undrilled	Javelins	Light Spear	7	4–6	4–12	
	Light Horse	Unprotected	Average	Undrilled	Bow	–	8	4–6	0–4	
Foot with javelins	Medium Foot	Protected	Average	Undrilled	–	Light Spear	5	6–8	0–32	
Foot with thrusting spear — Only before 250 BC	Medium Foot	Protected	Average	Undrilled	–	Offensive Spearmen	7	6–8	0–16	
"Swordsmen" — Only before 300 BC	Medium Foot	Protected	Average	Undrilled	–	Light Spear, Swordsmen	6	6–8	0–8	8–32
Foot with rhomphaia — From 350 to 251 BC	Medium Foot	Protected	Average	Undrilled	–	Heavy weapon	7	6–8	0–32	
Foot with rhomphaia — From 250 BC										
Skirmishers with javelins	Light Foot	Unprotected	Average	Undrilled	Javelins	Light Spear	4	6–8	0–8	
Skirmishers with bow	Light Foot	Unprotected	Average	Undrilled	Bow	–	5	6–8	0–8	
Skirmishers with sling	Light Foot	Unprotected	Average	Undrilled	Sling	–	4	6–8		

LYDIAN

This list covers the armies of the Lydian empire in western Asia Minor from the early 7th century BC until 546 BC when it was conquered by the Persians. Lydia was wealthy due to extensive gold deposits, and has been credited with the invention of coinage. The phrase "as rich as Croesus" refers to the last King of Lydia.

TROOP NOTES

Lydian heavy cavalry were armed with thrusting spears and had a sufficiently high reputation that the Persians, whose own cavalry were renowned for their quality and numbers, resorted to using camels to disrupt them.

LYDIAN STARTER ARMY

Commander-in-Chief	1	Field Commander
Sub-commanders	2	2 x Troop Commander
Lydian heavy cavalry	2 BGs	Each comprising 4 bases of heavy cavalry: Superior, Armoured, Undrilled Cavalry – Light Spear, Swordsmen
Lydian, Paphlagonian or Phrygian light horse	1 BG	4 bases of light horse: Average, Unprotected, Undrilled Light Horse – Javelins, Light Spear
Hoplites	4 BGs	Each comprising 6 bases of hoplites: Average, Armoured, Undrilled Heavy Foot – Offensive Spearmen
Lydian, Phrygian or Mysian javelinmen	3 BGs	Each comprising 6 bases of javelinmen: Average, Unprotected, Undrilled Light Foot – Javelins, Light Spear
Thracian "swordsmen"	1 BG	6 bases of Thracian "swordsmen": Average, Protected, Undrilled Medium Foot – Light Spear, Swordsmen
Camp	1	Unfortified camp
Total	11 BGs	Camp, 12 mounted bases, 48 foot bases, 3 commanders

BUILDING A CUSTOMISED LIST USING OUR ARMY POINTS

Choose an army based on the maxima and minima in the list below. The following special instructions apply to this army:

- Commanders should be depicted as heavy cavalry or chariots.
- Lydian heavy cavalry can always dismount if the enemy has camelry.

LYDIAN										
Territory Types: Agricultural, Hilly										
C-in-C	Inspired Commander/Field Commander/Troop Commander						80/50/35		1	
Sub-commanders	Field Commander						50		0–2	
	Troop Commander						35		0–3	
Troop name	Troop Type				Capabilities		Points per base	Bases per BG	Total bases	
	Type	Armour	Quality	Training	Shooting	Close Combat				
Core Troops										
Lydian heavy cavalry	Cavalry	Armoured	Superior	Undrilled	–	Light Spear, Swordsmen	16	4–6	6–24	
		Armoured		Drilled			17			
		Protected		Undrilled			12			
		Protected		Drilled			13			
Lydian, Paphlagonian or Phrygian light horse	Light Horse	Unprotected	Average	Undrilled	Javelins	Light Spear	7	4–6	4–12	
Lydian, Phrygian, Mysian, Thracian or similar foot with short spears or javelins	Medium Foot	Protected	Average	Undrilled	–	Light Spear	5	6–8	16–64	
	Light Foot	Unprotected	Average	Undrilled	Javelins	Light Spear	4	6–8		
Hoplites: Ionian or Karian mercenaries or Lydians	Heavy Foot	Armoured	Average	Undrilled	–	Offensive Spearmen	9	6–8	0–32	
				Drilled			10			
Optional Troops										
Chariots	Light chariots	–	Superior	Undrilled	–	Light Spear	15	4–6	0–8	
Skythian mercenaries	Light Horse or Cavalry	Unprotected	Average	Undrilled	Bow	Swordsmen	10	4	0–4	
Archers	Light Foot	Unprotected	Average	Undrilled	Bow	–	5	6–8	0–8	
Slingers	Light Foot	Unprotected	Average	Undrilled	Sling	–	4	6–8	0–8	
Thracian "swordsmen"	Medium Foot	Protected	Average	Undrilled	–	Light Spear, Swordsmen	6	4–6	0–6	
Special Campaigns										
Only in 546 BC										
Lydian foot recently upgraded to hoplites	Heavy Foot	Protected	Poor	Undrilled	–	Offensive Spearmen	5	6–8	0–24	

LATE DYNASTIC EGYPTIAN

This list covers Egyptian armies of the 26th dynasty from 664 BC to 525 BC, and the 28th, 29th and 30th dynasties from 405 BC to 343 BC. Psamtik I seceded from the Assyrian Empire c. 650 BC. Egypt was conquered by Cambyses II of Persia in 525 BC – forming the 27th dynasty – successfully revolted in 405 BC, then was reconquered by Artaxerxes III in 343 BC – forming the 31st dynasty.

TROOP NOTES

Large numbers of Greek mercenaries were used.

Mercenary Greek Hoplite

26TH DYNASTY EGYPTIAN STARTER ARMY		
Commander-in-Chief	1	Field Commander
Sub-commanders	2	2 x Troop Commander
Chariots	2 BGs	Each comprising 4 bases of chariots: Superior, Drilled Heavy Chariots – Bow
Cavalry	1 BG	4 bases of cavalry: Average, Unprotected, Undrilled Light Horse – Javelins, Light Spear
Mercenary Greek hoplites	2 BGs	Each comprising 6 bases of Greek hoplites: Average, Armoured, Drilled Heavy Foot – Offensive Spearmen
Egyptian spearmen	2 BGs	Each comprising 6 bases of Egyptian spearmen: Average, Protected, Drilled Heavy Foot – Defensive Spearmen
Egyptian archers	1 BG	6 bases of Egyptian archers: Average, Unprotected, Drilled Medium Foot – Bow
Nubian archers	1 BG	6 bases of Nubian archers: Superior, Unprotected, Undrilled Light Foot – Bow
Camp	1	Unfortified camp
Total	9 BGs	Camp, 12 mounted bases, 36 foot bases, 3 commanders

BUILDING A CUSTOMISED LIST USING OUR ARMY POINTS

Choose an army based on the maxima and minima in the list below. The following special instructions apply to this army:

- Egyptian commanders should be depicted as cavalry (but armoured) or chariots.
- Greek allied-commanders should be depicted as hoplites.
- Greek allied-commanders can only command hoplites.

LATE DYNASTIC EGYPTIAN

Territory Types: Agricultural, Developed

C-in-C		Inspired Commander/Field Commander/Troop Commander				80/50/35		1	
Sub-commanders		Field Commander				50		0–2	
		Troop Commander				35		0–3	
Greek allied commanders		Field Commander/Troop Commander				40/25		0–2	

Troop name		Troop Type				Capabilities		Points per base	Bases per BG	Total bases
		Type	Armour	Quality	Training	Shooting	Close Combat			
Core Troops										
Chariots	Only 26th dynasty	Heavy Chariots	–	Superior	Drilled	Bow	–	22	4–6	4–12
Cavalry		Light Horse	Unprotected	Average	Undrilled	Javelins	Light Spear	7	4–6	4–12
		Cavalry	Unprotected	Average	Undrilled	–	Light Spear	6	4–6	
Egyptian javelinmen	Only 26th dynasty before 570	Medium or Heavy Foot	Protected	Average	Drilled	–	Light Spear	6	6–8	12–66
				Poor				4		
Egyptian spearmen		Heavy Foot	Protected	Average	Drilled	–	Defensive Spearmen	7	6–8	
				Poor				5		
Egyptian archers		Medium Foot	Unprotected	Average	Drilled	Bow	–	6	6–8	6–32
				Poor				4		
Mercenary Greek hoplites	26th dynasty	Heavy Foot	Armoured	Average	Drilled	–	Offensive Spearmen	10	6–8	0–32
	28th – 30th dynasty	Heavy Foot	Protected	Average	Drilled	–	Offensive Spearmen	8	6–8	
Optional Troops										
Skythian mercenaries	Only 26th dynasty from 650	Light Horse or Cavalry	Unprotected	Average	Undrilled	Bow	Swordsmen	10	4	0–4
Guard spearmen		Heavy Foot	Protected	Superior	Drilled	–	Defensive Spearmen	9	4–6	0–6
Guard archers		Medium Foot	Unprotected	Superior	Drilled	Bow	–	7	4–6	
Libyan javelinmen		Light Foot	Unprotected	Average	Undrilled	Javelins	Light Spear	4	6–8	0–8
Nubian archers		Light Foot	Unprotected	Superior	Undrilled	Bow		6	6–8	0–12
				Average				5		
		Medium Foot	Unprotected	Superior	Undrilled	Bow	–	6	6–8	
				Average				5		
Allies										
Assyrian allies (Only 26th dynasty before 650) – Neo-Assyrian Empire										
Kyrenean Greek allies (Only from 570)										
Libyan allies (Only 30th dynasty from 360) – Late Libyan										

KYRENEAN GREEK

Kyrene was the oldest and most important of several Greek colonies on the coast of Libya. This list covers Kyrenean armies from the supposed date of foundation of the city as a colony of Thera circa 630 BC, until incorporation as a Roman province in 74 BC. After 322 BC, it was annexed to the Ptolemaic kingdom, although intermittently independent or semi-independent.

TROOP NOTES

Kyrenean chariots had 4 horses and probably 3 crewmen.

KYRENEAN GREEK STARTER ARMY

Commander-in-Chief	1	Field Commander
Sub-commanders	2	2 x Troop Commander
Chariots	2 BGs	Each comprising 4 bases of chariots: Superior, Undrilled Heavy Chariots – Light Spear
Cavalry	1 BG	4 bases of cavalry: Average, Armoured, Undrilled Cavalry – Light Spear
Hoplites	4 BGs	Each comprising 6 bases of Greek hoplites: Average, Armoured, Undrilled Heavy Foot – Offensive Spearmen
Javelinmen	2 BGs	Each comprising 6 bases of javelinmen: Average, Unprotected, Undrilled Light Foot – Javelins, Light Spear
Archers	1 BG	6 bases of archers: Average, Unprotected, Undrilled Light Foot - Bow
Camp	1	Unfortified camp
Total	10 BGs	Camp, 12 mounted bases, 42 foot bases, 3 commanders

BUILDING A CUSTOMISED LIST USING OUR ARMY POINTS

Choose an army based on the maxima and minima in the list below. The following special instructions apply to this army:

- Commanders should be depicted as chariots or cavalry.

Greek Hoplite

KYRENEAN GREEK

Territory Types: Agricultural, Desert

Troop name		Troop Type				Capabilities		Points per base	Bases per BG	Total bases
		Type	Armour	Quality	Training	Shooting	Close Combat			
C-in-C		Inspired Commander/Field Commander/Troop Commander						80/50/35	1	
Sub-commanders		Field Commander						50	0–2	
		Troop Commander						35	0–3	
Core Troops										
Chariots	Only before 275	Heavy Chariots	–	Superior	Undrilled	–	Light Spear	18	4–6	0–12
Cavalry		Cavalry	Armoured	Average	Undrilled	–	Light Spear	10	4–6	0–6
			Protected					7		
Xystophoroi	Only from 321	Cavalry	Armoured	Superior	Drilled	–	Lancers, Swordsmen	17	4–6	
				Average				13		
Hoplites	Before 460	Heavy Foot	Armoured	Average	Undrilled	–	Offensive Spearmen	9	6–8	24–100
	From 490	Heavy Foot	Protected	Average	Undrilled	–	Offensive Spearmen	7	6–8	
Javelinmen		Light Foot	Unprotected	Average	Undrilled	Javelins	Light Spear	4	6–8	6–32
				Poor				2		
Optional Troops										
Archers		Light Foot	Unprotected	Average	Undrilled or Drilled	Bow	–	5	6–8	0–8
Slingers		Light Foot	Unprotected	Average	Undrilled	Sling	–	4	6–8	0–8
Phalangites	Only from 321	Heavy Foot	Protected	Average	Drilled	–	Pikemen	6	8–12	0–12
Cretans	Only from 321	Light Foot	Unprotected	Superior	Drilled	Bow	–	6	6–8	0–8
Upgrade hoplites to mercenaries:	Only from 313 to 308	Heavy Foot	Protected	Average	Drilled	–	Offensive Spearmen	8	6–8	8–24
Thureophoroi	Only from 279	Medium Foot or Heavy Foot	Protected	Average	Drilled	–	Offensive Spearmen	8	4–6	0–6
Allies										
Carthaginian allies (Only in 322) – Early Carthaginian										
Libyan allies – Late Libyan										

KYRENEAN GREEK ALLIES

Allied commander		Field Commander/Troop Commander					40/25		1	
Troop name		Troop Type				Capabilities		Points per base	Bases per BG	Total bases
		Type	Armour	Quality	Training	Shooting	Close Combat			
Core Troops										
Chariots	Only before 275	Heavy Chariots	–	Superior	Undrilled	–	Light Spear	18	4	0–4
Cavalry		Cavalry	Armoured	Average	Undrilled	–	Light Spear	10	4	0–4
			Protected					7		
Xystophoroi	Only from 321	Cavalry	Armoured	Superior	Drilled	–	Lancers, Swordsmen	17	4	
				Average				13		
Hoplites	Before 460	Heavy Foot	Armoured	Average	Undrilled	–	Offensive Spearmen	9	6–8	8–32
	From 490	Heavy Foot	Protected	Average	Undrilled	–	Offensive Spearmen	7	6–8	
Javelinmen		Light Foot	Unprotected	Average	Undrilled	Javelins	Light Spear	4	6–8	0–12
				Poor				2		
Upgrade hoplites to mercenaries:	Only from 313 to 308	Heavy Foot	Protected	Average	Drilled	–	Offensive Spearmen	8	6–8	8–24

LATE LIBYAN ALLIES

This list covers Libyan allied contingents from 550 BC.

TROOP NOTES

Libyan chariots had 4 horses and 1 or 2 crewmen with spears. When Agathokles of Syracuse was campaigning in Africa with 13,500 men in 307 BC, he was joined by a Libyan allied contingent of 10,000 infantry and 6,000 chariots.

- The commander should be depicted as chariots.

LATE LIBYAN ALLIES

Allied commander		Field Commander/Troop Commander					40/25		1	
Troop name		Troop Type				Capabilities		Points per base	Bases per BG	Total bases
		Type	Armour	Quality	Training	Shooting	Close Combat			
Chariots		Light Chariots	–	Superior	Undrilled	–	Light Spear	15	4–6	0–18
				Average				11		
Javelinmen		Light Foot	Unprotected	Average	Undrilled	Javelins	Light Spear	4	6–8	16–48

EARLY CARTHAGINIAN

Carthage, on the North African coast near modern Tunis, was a colony of the Phoenician city of Tyre. The traditional date of its foundation is 814 BC, but not much is known about its army in the earliest period. This list covers Carthaginian armies from the start of the Magonid dynasty, circa 550 BC, until 275 BC. During this period Carthage gained a maritime empire in the western Mediterranean, and fought many wars against the Greek cities of Sicily.

TROOP NOTES

From the limited evidence available, it is possible that the Carthaginian four-horse chariots were bow-armed. However, in view of the apparent lack of any archery tradition in Carthage, we also allow for the alternative that they were spear or javelin-armed.

Poeni Cavalryman

EARLY CARTHAGINIAN STARTER ARMY		
Commander-in-Chief	1	Field Commander
Sub-commanders	2	2 x Troop Commander
Chariots	2 BGs	Each comprising 4 bases of chariots: Superior, Drilled Heavy Chariots – Bow
Numidian light cavalry	1 BG	4 bases of Numidian light cavalry: Average, Unprotected, Undrilled Light Horse – Javelins, Light Spear
Sacred Band	1 BG	6 bases of Sacred Band: Superior, Armoured, Drilled Heavy Foot – Offensive Spearmen
African spearmen	2 BGs	Each comprising 6 bases of African spearmen: Average, Protected, Drilled Heavy Foot – Offensive Spearmen
Spanish scutarii	1 BG	6 bases of Spanish scutarii: Average, Protected, Undrilled Medium Foot – Impact Foot, Swordsmen
Ligurian foot	1 BG	6 bases of Ligurian foot: Average, Protected, Undrilled Medium Foot – Light Spear
Numidian javelinmen	1 BG	6 bases of javelinmen: Average, Unprotected, Undrilled Light Foot – Javelins, Light Spear
Camp	1	Unfortified camp
Total	9 BGs	Camp, 12 mounted bases, 36 foot bases, 3 commanders

BUILDING A CUSTOMISED LIST USING OUR ARMY POINTS

Choose an army based on the maxima and minima in the list below. The following special instructions apply to this army:

- Commanders should be depicted as chariots or Poeni cavalry.
- All Poeni chariots must have the same combat capabilities.

Balearic Slinger

Carthaginian Standard-bearer, Sacred Band, by Richard Hook. Taken from Men-at-Arms 121:
Armies of the Carthaginian Wars 265–146 BC.

EARLY CARTHAGINIAN

Territory Types: Agricultural, Developed

C-in-C	Inspired Commander/Field Commander/Troop Commander				80/50/35	1	
Sub-commanders	Field Commander				50	0–2	
	Troop Commander				35	0–3	

Troop name	Troop Type				Capabilities		Points per base	Bases per BG	Total bases
	Type	Armour	Quality	Training	Shooting	Close Combat			
Core Troops									
Poeni chariots	Heavy Chariots	–	Superior	Drilled	Bow	–	22	4–6	0–12
	Heavy Chariots	–	Superior	Drilled	–	Light Spear	20		
Poeni cavalry	Cavalry	Armoured	Average	Drilled	–	Light Spear	11	4–6	0–6
		Protected					8		
Campanian, Etruscan or Greek cavalry	Only from 410	Cavalry	Armoured	Average	Drilled	–	Light Spear, Swordsmen	13	4–6	0–12
			Protected					10		
Numidian light cavalry	Only from 340	Light Horse	Unprotected	Average	Undrilled	Javelins	Light Spear	7	4–6	0–6
Sacred Band	Heavy Foot	Armoured	Superior	Drilled	–	Offensive Spearmen	13	6–8	0–8
African spearmen	Heavy Foot	Protected	Average	Drilled	–	Offensive Spearmen	8	6–8	12–24
			Poor				6		
Numidian, Libyan, Moorish or Spanish javelinmen	Light Foot	Unprotected	Average	Undrilled	Javelins	Light Spear	4	6–8	6–12
Corsican, Ligurian or Sardinian foot	Medium Foot	Protected	Average	Undrilled	–	Light Spear	5	6–8	6–24
Optional Troops									
Greek mercenary hoplites	Only from 410	Heavy Foot	Protected	Average	Drilled	–	Offensive Spearmen	8	6–8	0–16
Other Poeni foot	Heavy Foot	Protected	Average	Drilled	–	Offensive Spearmen	8	6–8	0–8
	Medium Foot	Protected	Average	Drilled	–	Light Spear, Swordsmen	7	6–8	
Poeni or other emergency levies	Medium Foot	Protected	Poor	Drilled	–	Light Spear, Swordsmen	5	6–8	0–24
Spanish scutarii	Medium Foot	Protected	Average	Undrilled	–	Impact foot, Swordsmen	7	6–8	0–8
Gallic foot	Only from 410	Heavy Foot	Protected	Average	Undrilled	–	Impact Foot, Swordsmen	7	6–8	0–8
Campanian mercenaries	Heavy Foot	Protected	Average	Drilled	–	Offensive Spearmen	8	6–8	0–8
	Medium Foot	Protected	Average	Drilled	–	Light Spear, Swordsmen	7	6–8	
Balearic slingers	Light Foot	Unprotected	Superior	Undrilled	Slings	–	5	4–6	0–6
Sardinian archers	Light Foot	Unprotected	Average	Undrilled	Bow	–	5	4	0–4
Bolt-shooters	Only from 390	Heavy Artillery	–	Average	Drilled	Heavy Artillery	–	20	2	0–2
Allies									
Libyan allies (Only before 500) – Late Libyan									
Numidian allies (Only from 340) – See Field of Glory Companion 1: *Rise of Rome: Republican Rome at War*									

EARLY CARTHAGINIAN ALLIES

Allied commander		Field Commander/Troop Commander					40/25		1
Troop name		Troop Type				Capabilities		Points per base	Bases per BG	Total bases
		Type	Armour	Quality	Training	Shooting	Close Combat			
Poeni chariots		Heavy Chariots	–	Superior	Drilled	Bow	–	22	4	0–4
		Heavy Chariots	–	Superior	Drilled	–	Light Spear	20		
Poeni cavalry		Cavalry	Armoured	Average	Drilled	–	Light Spear	11	4	
			Protected					8		
Campanian, Etruscan or Greek cavalry	Only from 410	Cavalry	Armoured	Average	Drilled	–	Light Spear, Swordsmen	13	4	0–4
			Protected					10		
Numidian light cavalry	Only from 340	Light Horse	Unprotected	Average	Undrilled	Javelins	Light Spear	7	4	
African spearmen		Heavy Foot	Protected	Average	Drilled	–	Offensive Spearmen	8	6–8	6–8
				Poor				6		
Numidian, Libyan, Moorish or Spanish javelinmen		Light Foot	Unprotected	Average	Undrilled	Javelins	Light Spear	4	4–6	4–6
Corsican, Ligurian or Sardinian foot		Medium Foot	Protected	Average	Undrilled	–	Light Spear	5	4–8	4–8

SKYTHIAN OR SAKA

This list covers Skythian and Saka armies from 550 BC until 50 AD. Saka were the eastern tribes, including the Massagetae, the Dahae (including the Parni who became the Parthians) and the Yueh-chi prior to their conquest of the Graeco-Bactrian kingdom c.130 BC.

TROOP NOTES

The sagaris, a horseman's axe with compact but heavy head, and a shaft up to 3 foot long, we treat as equivalent to sword when used on horseback. The Seleucid pikemen in 129 BC represent the army of Antigonos VII which was captured by the Parthians then changed sides when the Parthians attempted to use them against the Saka.

SAKA STARTER ARMY

Commander-in-Chief	1	Field Commander
Sub-commanders	2	2 x Troop Commander
Armoured cavalry	3 BGs	Each comprising 4 bases of armoured cavalry: Superior, Heavily Armoured, Undrilled Cataphracts – Lancers, Swordsmen
Unarmoured cavalry	2 BGs	Each comprising 4 bases of unarmoured cavalry: Average, Unprotected, Undrilled Cavalry – Bow, Swordsmen
Unarmoured cavalry	3 BGs	Each comprising 4 bases of unarmoured cavalry: Average, Unprotected, Undrilled Light Horse – Bow, Swordsmen
Foot archers	2 BGs	Each comprising 6 bases of foot archers: Poor, Unprotected, Undrilled Light Foot – Bow
Foot spearmen	1 BG	8 bases of foot spearmen: Poor, Protected, Undrilled Medium Foot – Light Spear
Camp	1	Unfortified camp
Total	11 BGs	Camp, 32 mounted bases, 20 foot bases, 3 commanders

BUILDING A CUSTOMISED LIST USING OUR ARMY POINTS

Choose an army based on the maxima and minima in the list below. The following special instructions apply to this army:

- Commanders should be depicted as armoured cavalry.
- Minima marked * apply if any non-allied foot are used.

Armoured Skythian warrior, 5th Century BC, by Angus McBride. Taken from Men-at-Arms 137: The Scythians 700–300 BC.

SKYTHIAN OR SAKA

Territory Types: Steppes

C-in-C	Inspired Commander/Field Commander/Troop Commander					80/50/35	1	
Sub-commanders	Field Commander					50	0–2	
	Troop Commander					35	0–3	

Troop name		Troop Type				Capabilities		Points per base	Bases per BG	Total bases
		Type	Armour	Quality	Training	Shooting	Close Combat			
Core Troops										
Armoured cavalry	Only before 300 BC	Cavalry	Armoured	Superior	Undrilled	Bow	Swordsmen	18	4–6	0–12
	Only from 300 BC	Cavalry	Armoured	Superior	Undrilled	–	Lancers, Swordsmen	16	4–6	
	Only Saka from 250 BC	Cataphracts	Heavily Armoured	Superior	Undrilled	–	Lancers, Swordsmen	18	4–6	
Unarmoured cavalry		Light Horse or Cavalry	Unprotected	Average	Undrilled	Bow	Swordsmen	10	4–6	20–72
Foot archers	Any	Light Foot	Unprotected	Average	Undrilled	Bow	–	5	6–8	*12–24
				Poor				3		
		Medium Foot	Unprotected	Average	Undrilled	Bow	–	5	6–8	
				Poor				3		
	Only before 300 BC	Medium Foot	Unprotected	Average	Undrilled	Bow	Light Spear	5	1/2	6–8
		Medium Foot	Unprotected	Average	Undrilled	Bow	–	5	1/2	
		Medium Foot	Unprotected	Poor	Undrilled	Bow	Light Spear	3	1/2	6–8
		Medium Foot	Unprotected	Poor	Undrilled	Bow	–	3	1/2	
Foot spearmen		Medium Foot	Protected	Average	Undrilled	–	Light Spear	5	6–8	*8–24
				Poor				3		
Optional Troops										
Slingers		Light Foot	Unprotected	Average	Undrilled	Sling	–	4	4–6	0–6
				Poor				2		
Allies										
Mountain Indian allies (Only Saka)										
Special Campaigns										
Only Skythians in 313 BC										
Thracian allies										
Black Sea Greek allies – Classical Greek										
Only Saka in 129 BC										
Seleucid pikemen		Heavy Foot	Protected	Average	Drilled	–	Pikemen	6	8–12	0–12
				Poor				4		

Skythian king and armoured nobleman, by Angus McBride. Taken from Men-at-Arms 137:
The Scythians 700–300 BC.

EARLY SKYTHIAN OR SAKA ALLIES

This covers Skythian or Saka allied contingents prior to 300 BC.

- Commanders should be depicted as armoured cavalry.

EARLY SKYTHIAN OR SAKA ALLIES									
Allied commander	Field Commander/Troop Commander						40/25	1	
Troop name	Troop Type				Capabilities		Points per base	Bases per BG	Total bases
	Type	Armour	Quality	Training	Shooting	Close Combat			
Armoured cavalry	Cavalry	Armoured	Superior	Undrilled	Bow	Swordsmen	18	4	0–4
Unarmoured cavalry	Light Horse or Cavalry	Unprotected	Average	Undrilled	Bow	Swordsmen	10	4–6	6–18
Foot archers	Light Foot	Unprotected	Average	Undrilled	Bow	–	5	6–8	0–8
			Poor				3		
	Medium Foot	Unprotected	Average	Undrilled	Bow	–	5	6–8	
			Poor				3		
	Medium Foot	Unprotected	Average	Undrilled	Bow	Light Spear	5	1/2	
	Medium Foot	Unprotected	Average	Undrilled	Bow	–	5	1/2	6–8
	Medium Foot	Unprotected	Poor	Undrilled	Bow	Light Spear	3	1/2	
	Medium Foot	Unprotected	Poor	Undrilled	Bow	–	3	1/2	6–8
Foot spearmen	Medium Foot	Protected	Average	Undrilled	–	Light Spear	5	6–8	0–8
			Poor				3		

CLASSICAL INDIAN

This list covers the armies of northern and central India from 500 BC until the fall of the Guptas in the mid-5th century AD.

TROOP NOTES

Alexander's admiral, Nearchos, states that all Indian infantry carried a large two-handed sword, used for powerful downward cutting blows. However, Indian art shows many infantry with smaller swords and the Arthasastra describes 3 types of swords, only one of which seems likely to have been two-handed. We assume that a variety of swords were in use, and classify the mixture for close combat capability purposes as swordsmen, although Nearchos does note that Indian infantry were not eager to advance to close combat. Armour for infantry became more common in the 1st century AD, but evidence of determined swordsmanship is then lacking.

Indian shielded javelinnmen may sometimes have formed up in front of the archers. However, as

Indian Archer

they are unlikely to have been more than a rank or two, and as both javelinmen and archers were largely unarmoured, this is not enough to qualify the combined formation as Protected.

Most states (including the Mauryan and Gupta empires) were ruled by kings, but some were republics and lacked the resources to field war elephants.

CLASSICAL INDIAN STARTER ARMY		
Commander-in-Chief	1	Field Commander
Sub-commanders	2	2 x Troop Commander
Elephants	3 BGs	Each comprising 2 bases of elephants: Average, Undrilled Elephants
Heavy chariots	1 BG	4 bases of heavy chariots: Superior, Undrilled Heavy Chariots - Bow
Cavalry	1 BG	4 bases of cavalry: Average, Unprotected, Undrilled Cavalry – Light Spear
Archers	3 BGs	Each comprising 8 bases of archers: Average, Unprotected, Undrilled Medium Foot – Bow, Swordsmen
Javelinmen	2 BGs	Each comprising 6 bases of javelinmen: Average, Protected, Undrilled Medium Foot – Light Spear, Swordsmen
Camp	1	Unfortified camp
Total	10 BGs	Camp, 14 mounted bases, 36 foot bases, 3 commanders

BUILDING A CUSTOMISED LIST USING OUR ARMY POINTS

Choose an army based on the maxima and minima in the list below. The following special instructions apply to this army:

- Commanders should be depicted as elephants, chariots or cavalry.
- An Indian allied general's contingent must conform to the Classical Indian allies list below, but the troops in the contingent are deducted from the minima and maxima in the main list.
- The Mauryas from 321 to 180 BC can have drilled chariots, cavalry, archers and javelinmen. If any non-allied troops of any of these types are drilled, all must be. Indian allied contingents in a Mauryan army must be undrilled. Other states in this period can have one Mauryan allied contingent, which can be drilled.

Indian Elephant

CLASSICAL INDIAN

Territory Types: Agricultural, Woodlands, Tropical

C-in-C	Inspired Commander/Field Commander/Troop Commander					80/50/35	1	
Sub-commanders	Field Commander/Troop Commander					50/35	0–2	
Indian allied commanders	Field Commander/Troop Commander					40/25	0–3	

Troop name		Troop Type				Capabilities		Points per base	Bases per BG	Total bases
		Type	Armour	Quality	Training	Shooting	Close Combat			
Core Troops										
Elephants	Only non-republican states	Elephants	–	Average	Undrilled	–	–	25	2	2–12
Heavy chariots	Any	Heavy chariots	–	Superior	Undrilled	Bow	–	20	4–6	0–8
	Only Mauryas from 321 to 180 BC	Heavy chariots	–	Superior	Drilled	Bow	–	22	4–6	
Light chariots	Any	Light chariots	–	Superior	Undrilled	Bow	–	17	4–6	
	Only Mauryas from 321 to 180 BC	Light chariots	–	Superior	Drilled	Bow	–	18	4–6	
Cavalry	Any	Cavalry	Unprotected	Average	Undrilled	–	Light Spear	6	4–6	4–18
			Unprotected	Poor				4		
			Protected	Average				7		
			Protected	Poor				5		
	Only Mauryas from 321 to 180 BC	Cavalry	Unprotected	Average	Drilled	–	Light Spear	7	4–6	
			Unprotected	Poor				5		
			Protected	Average				8		
			Protected	Poor				6		
Archers	Any before 1 AD	Medium Foot	Unprotected	Average	Undrilled	Bow	Swordsmen	6	6–8	24–112
				Poor				4		
	Only Mauryas from 321 to 180 BC	Medium Foot	Unprotected	Average	Drilled	Bow	Swordsmen	7	6–8	
				Poor				5		
	Any from 1 AD	Medium Foot	Unprotected	Average	Undrilled	Bow	–	5	6–8	
			Unprotected	Poor				3		
			Protected	Average				6		
			Protected	Poor				4		
Javelinmen	Any	Medium Foot	Protected	Average	Undrilled	–	Light Spear, Swordsmen	6	6–8	6–24
				Poor				4		
	Only Mauryas from 321 to 180 BC	Medium Foot	Protected	Average	Drilled	–	Light Spear, Swordsmen	7	6–8	
				Poor				5		
Optional Troops										
Forest tribesmen		Light Foot	Unprotected	Average	Undrilled	Bow	–	5	4–6	0–6
				Poor				3		
Clubmen		Medium Foot	Unprotected	Average	Undrilled	–	Heavy weapon	6	4	0–4
			Protected					7		
Horse archers	Only from 179 BC	Light Horse	Unprotected	Average	Undrilled	Bow	Swordsmen	10	4	0–4
		Light Horse	Unprotected	Average	Undrilled	Bow	–	8		
Upgrade cavalry to armoured lancers	Only Guptas from 320 AD	Cavalry	Armoured	Superior	Undrilled	–	Lancers, Swordsmen	16	4–6	4–6
Replace elephants and/or chariots by bullock or camel carts		Battle Wagons	–	Poor	Undrilled	Bow	–	11	2–4	0–6
Artillery		Light Artillery	–	Average	Undrilled	Light Artillery	–	15	2	0–2
		Heavy Artillery	–	Average	Undrilled	Heavy Artillery	–	20		
Fortified camp								24		0–1

CLASSICAL INDIAN ALLIES

Allied commander			Field Commander/Troop Commander				40/25		1	
Troop name		Troop Type				Capabilities		Points per base	Bases per BG	Total bases
		Type	Armour	Quality	Training	Shooting	Close Combat			
Elephants	Only non-republican states	Elephants	–	Average	Undrilled	–	–	25	2	2–4
Heavy chariots	Any	Heavy chariots	–	Superior	Undrilled	Bow	–	20	4–6	0–4
	Only Mauryas from 321 to 180 BC	Heavy chariots	–	Superior	Drilled	Bow	–	22	4–6	
Light chariots	Any	Light chariots	–	Superior	Undrilled	Bow	–	17	4–6	
	Only Mauryas from 321 to 180 BC	Light chariots	–	Superior	Drilled	Bow	–	18	4–6	
Cavalry	Any	Cavalry	Unprotected	Average	Undrilled	–	Light Spear	6	4–6	0–6
			Unprotected	Poor				4		
			Protected	Average				7		
			Protected	Poor				5		
	Only Mauryas from 321 to 180 BC	Cavalry	Unprotected	Average	Drilled	–	Light Spear	7	4–6	
			Unprotected	Poor				5		
			Protected	Average				8		
			Protected	Poor				6		
Archers	Any before 1 AD	Medium Foot	Unprotected	Average	Undrilled	Bow	Swordsmen	6	6–8	6–24
				Poor				4		
	Only Mauryas from 321 to 180 BC	Medium Foot	Unprotected	Average	Drilled	Bow	Swordsmen	7	6–8	
				Poor				5		
	Any from 1 AD	Medium Foot	Unprotected	Average	Undrilled	Bow	–	5	6–8	
			Unprotected	Poor				4		
			Protected	Average				6		
			Protected	Poor				5		
Javelinmen	Any	Medium Foot	Protected	Average	Undrilled	–	Light Spear, Swordsmen	6	6–8	0–8
				Poor				4		
	Only Mauryas from 321 to 180 BC	Medium Foot	Protected	Average	Drilled	–	Light Spear, Swordsmen	7	6–8	
				Poor				5		

MOUNTAIN INDIAN ALLIES

Allied commander		Field Commander/Troop Commander				40/25		1	
Troop name		Troop Type				Capabilities		Points per base	Bases per BG	Total bases
	Type	Armour	Quality	Training	Shooting	Close Combat			
Cavalry	Light Horse	Unprotected	Average	Undrilled	Javelins	Light Spear	7	4–6	0–6
Spearmen	Medium Foot	Protected	Average	Undrilled	-	Light Spear	5	6–8	6–18
Archers	Light Foot	Unprotected	Average	Undrilled	Bow	-	5	6–8	6–18
	Medium Foot	Unprotected	Average	Undrilled	Bow	-	5		

LATE ACHAEMENID PERSIAN

This list covers Achaemenid Persian armies from 420 BC until the completion of Alexander the Great's conquest of the empire in 329 BC.

TROOP NOTES

One interpretation of the enigmatic "Kardakes" is that they were Persians equipped and trained as hoplites. They may, alternatively, have been the lighter peltast-style spearmen with crescent shields.

Although most of the heavy cavalry seem to have switched from bow to javelins around the start of this period, some may have retained bows right up to the end of the empire. The most likely to have done so would be the Bactrians and Saka.

LATE ACHAEMENID PERSIAN STARTER ARMY		
Commander-in-Chief	1	1 x Troop Commander (Darius III)
Sub-commanders	2	2 x Troop Commander
Bactrian and Saka heavy cavalry	2 BGs	Each comprising 4 bases of heavy cavalry: Superior, Armoured, Undrilled Cavalry – Bow, Swordsmen
Persian and Median heavy cavalry	2 BGs	Each comprising 4 bases of heavy cavalry: Average, Armoured, Undrilled Cavalry – Light Spear, Swordsmen
Arachosian and Paphlagonian light horse	1 BG	6 bases of light horse: Average, Unprotected, Undrilled Cavalry – Javelins, Light Spear
Greek or Persian hoplites	2 BGs	Each comprising 8 bases of hoplites: Average, Protected, Drilled Heavy Foot – Offensive Spearmen
Persian crescent shield spearmen	1 BG	6 bases of crescent shield spearmen: Average, Protected, Undrilled Medium Foot – Light Spear
Archers	1 BG	6 bases of archers: Average, Unprotected, Undrilled Light Foot – Bow
Slingers	1 BG	6 bases of slingers: Average, Unprotected, Undrilled Light Foot – Sling
Camp	1	Unfortified camp
Total	10 BGs	Camp, 22 mounted bases, 34 foot bases, 3 commanders

BUILDING A CUSTOMISED LIST USING OUR ARMY POINTS

Choose an army based on the maxima and minima in the list below. The following special instructions apply to this army:

- The C-in-C should be depicted as guard cavalry or a light chariot.
- Commanders should be depicted as guard cavalry.
- Lykian allies cannot be used with guard infantry or elephants.

Persian Archer

LATE ACHAEMENID PERSIAN

Territory Types: Agricultural, Developed, Hilly

C-in-C	Inspired Commander/Field Commander/Troop Commander					80/50/35	1	
Sub-commanders	Field Commander					50	0–2	
	Troop Commander					35	0–3	

Troop name	Troop Type				Capabilities		Points per base	Bases per BG	Total bases
	Type	Armour	Quality	Training	Shooting	Close Combat			
Core Troops									
Persian, Median, Armenian, Bactrian, Saka, Kappadokian or other heavy cavalry	Cavalry	Armoured	Superior	Undrilled	–	Light Spear, Swordsmen	16	4–6	8–42
		Armoured	Average				12		
		Armoured	Poor				9		
		Protected	Superior				12		
		Protected	Average				9		
		Protected	Poor				7		12–42
	Cavalry	Armoured	Superior	Undrilled	Bow	Swordsmen	18	4–6	0–8
		Armoured	Average				14		
		Armoured	Poor				11		
		Protected	Superior				14		
		Protected	Average				11		
		Protected	Poor				9		
Arachosian, Paphlagonian or similar light horse	Light Horse	Unprotected	Average	Undrilled	Javelins	Light Spear	7	4–6	6–12
Archers	Light Foot	Unprotected	Average	Undrilled	Bow	–	5	6–8	0–12	0–18
Slingers	Light Foot	Unprotected	Average	Undrilled	Sling	–	4	6–8	0–12
Optional Troops									
Guard cavalry	Cavalry	Armoured	Elite	Drilled	–	Light Spear, Swordsmen	20	2–4	0–4
Bactrian light horse	Light Horse	Unprotected	Average	Undrilled	Bow	Light Spear	9	4–6	0–6
Parthyaian or similar horse archers	Light Horse	Unprotected	Average	Undrilled	Bow	–	8	4–6	0–6
Saka horse archers	Light Horse or Cavalry	Unprotected	Average	Undrilled	Bow	Swordsmen	10	4–6	0–6
Guard infantry ("Apple bearers")	Heavy Foot	Protected	Elite	Drilled	–	Offensive spearmen	12	1/2	4	0–4
	Medium Foot	Protected	Elite	Drilled	Bow	–	11	1/2	
	Heavy Foot	Protected	Superior	Drilled	–	Offensive spearmen	10	1/2	4
	Medium Foot	Protected	Superior	Drilled	Bow	–	9	1/2	
Persian crescent shield spearmen	Medium Foot	Protected	Average	Undrilled	–	Light Spear	5	6–8	0–24
				Drilled			6		
Asiatic Greek or Persian hoplites	Heavy Foot	Protected	Average	Drilled	–	Offensive Spearmen	8	6–8	0–24	0–32
			Poor				6		
Mercenary or allied Greek hoplites	Heavy Foot	Protected	Average	Drilled	–	Offensive Spearmen	8	6–8	0–32
Mercenary Greek peltasts	Light Foot	Unprotected	Average	Drilled	Javelins	Light Spear	4	4	0–4
Egyptian spearmen	Heavy Foot	Protected	Poor	Drilled	–	Defensive Spearmen	5	4–6	0–6
Hillmen	Medium Foot	Protected	Average	Undrilled	–	Light Spear	5	6–8	0–8
	Light Foot	Unprotected	Average	Undrilled	Javelins	Light Spear	4	6–8	

Thracians	Medium Foot	Protected	Average	Undrilled	–	Light Spear	5	4	0–4
	Medium Foot	Protected	Average	Undrilled	–	Offensive spearmen	7	4	
	Medium Foot	Protected	Average	Undrilled	–	Light Spear, Swordsmen	6	4	
Chalybes	Medium Foot	Unprotected	Average	Undrilled	–	Defensive spearmen	5	4	0–4
Massed levies	Mob	Unprotected	Poor	Undrilled	–	–	2	8–12	0–24
Scythed chariots	Scythed Chariots	–	Average	Undrilled	–	–	15	2–4	0–4
Fortified camp							24		0–1
Allies									
Lykian allies									
Special Campaigns									
Only Darius III at Gaugamela in 331									
Upgrade guard cavalry to	Cavalry	Armoured	Elite	Drilled	–	Lancers, Swordsmen	20	2–4	All
Elephants	Elephants	–	Average	Undrilled	–	–	25	2	2
Cannot use Egyptians, Thracians or Lykian allies, nor more than 8 bases of hoplites. Guard cavalry and infantry are compulsory.									
Only Bessos in 329									
Saka allies									
Cannot use hoplites, peltasts, scythed chariots, Egyptians, Thracians or Lykian allies.									

SYRACUSAN

Syracuse, on the south east coast of Sicily, was founded c.733 BC by Greek settlers from Corinth and Tenea. For early Syracusan armies, use the Classical Greek list. This list covers Syracuse's armies from 412 BC, following the defeat of the Athenian Sicilian Expedition, until the city fell to the Romans in 211 BC.

Through most of the period Syracuse was the dominant power in eastern Sicily, while Carthage

Citizen Hoplite

controlled the west. The two states were in frequent conflict. In the early 4th century BC, Syracuse briefly also controlled the southern coast of the Italian mainland. During the First Punic War, she came into conflict with Rome, but sensibly sued for peace early on. In the Second Punic War, she allied with Carthage, thus sealing her own fate. After a three-year siege, the city was captured and sacked by the Romans. During the siege, Archimedes, the great Syracusan mathematician and engineer, devised various "secret weapons" that were used in the defence of the city. These included his famous "death ray", used to set fire to Roman ships by focusing the rays of the sun with mirrors, and the "ship shaker" which used a claw on a crane to capsize them. Recent modern experiments have attempted to duplicate these weapons, and have pronounced them feasible. Archimedes was killed during the sack of the city.

SYRACUSAN STARTER ARMY

Commander-in-Chief	1	Field Commander
Sub-commanders	2	2 x Troop Commander
Greek or Campanian cavalry	2 BGs	Each comprising 4 bases of cavalry: Superior, Armoured, Drilled Cavalry – Light Spear, Swordsmen
Syracusan citizen hoplites	2 BGs	Each comprising 6 bases of hoplites: Average, Protected, Undrilled Heavy Foot – Offensive Spearmen
Greek mercenary hoplites	2 BGs	Each comprising 6 bases of hoplites: Average, Protected, Drilled Heavy Foot – Offensive Spearmen
Mercenary thurophoroi	1 BG	6 bases of thureophoroi: Average, Protected, Drilled Medium Foot – Offensive Spearmen
Spanish mercenary scutarii	1 BG	6 bases of Spanish scutarii: Average, Protected, Undrilled Medium Foot – Impact Foot, Swordsmen
Slingers	2 BGs	Each comprising 6 bases of slingers: Average, Unprotected, Undrilled Light Foot – Sling
Javelinmen	1 BG	6 bases of javelinmen: Average, Unprotected, Undrilled Light Foot – Javelins, Light Spear
Camp	1	Unfortified camp
Total	11 BGs	Camp, 8 mounted bases, 54 foot bases, 3 commanders

BUILDING A CUSTOMISED LIST USING OUR ARMY POINTS

Choose an army based on the maxima and minima in the list below. The following special instructions apply to this army:

- Commanders should be depicted as cavalry or hoplites.
- It is permissable to depict the disguised rowers by using hoplites. If this is done, their true nature need not be disclosed until they are shot at or engaged in close combat.

Mercenary Hoplite, by Adam Hook.
Taken from Warrior 27: Greek Hoplite 480–323 BC.

SYRACUSAN

Territory Types: Agricultural, Developed

Troop name		Troop Type			Capabilities		Points per base	Bases per BG	Total bases
C-in-C		Inspired Commander/Field Commander/Troop Commander					80/50/35	1	
Sub-commanders		Field Commander					50	0–2	
		Troop Commander					35	0–3	
Troop name		Type	Armour	Quality	Training	Shooting	Close Combat	Points per base	Bases per BG	Total bases

Troop name	Type	Armour	Quality	Training	Shooting	Close Combat	Points per base	Bases per BG	Total bases
Core Troops									
Greek cavalry	Cavalry	Armoured	Superior	Drilled	–	Light Spear, Swordsmen	17	4–6	4–12
			Average				13		4–12
Campanian cavalry	Cavalry	Armoured	Superior	Drilled	–	Light Spear, Swordsmen	17	4–6	0–6
Citizen hoplites	Heavy Foot	Protected	Average	Undrilled		Offensive Spearmen	7	6–8	12–24
			Average	Drilled			8		
			Poor	Undrilled			5		
			Poor	Drilled			6		
Greek mercenary hoplites	Heavy Foot	Protected	Average	Drilled	–	Offensive Spearmen	8	6–8	12–24
Archers	Light foot	Unprotected	Average	Undrilled or Drilled	Bow	–	5	6–8	0–12
Slingers	Light foot	Unprotected	Average	Undrilled or Drilled	Sling	–	4	6–8	0–12
6–18									
Optional Troops									
Tarentines	Light Horse	Unprotected	Average	Drilled	Javelins	Light Spear	7	4–6	0–6
Tyrant's mercenary bodyguard hoplites	Heavy Foot	Protected	Superior	Drilled	–	Offensive Spearmen	10	4–6	0–6
Campanian or Etruscan mercenary hoplites	Heavy Foot	Protected	Average	Drilled	–	Offensive Spearmen	8	6–8	0–12
Gallic mercenaries	Heavy Foot	Protected	Average	Undrilled	–	Impact Foot, Swordsmen	7	6–12	0–12
Samnite or similar Italian mercenaries	Medium Foot	Protected	Average	Drilled	–	Light Spear, Swordsmen	7	6–8	0–12
Mercenary peltasts — Only before 275	Light Foot	Unprotected	Average	Drilled	Javelins	Light Spear	4	6–8	0–6
Other javelinmen	Light Foot	Unprotected	Average	Undrilled	Javelins	Light Spear	4	6–8	0–16
			Poor				2		
0–16									
Mercenary thureophoroi — Only from 275	Medium Foot or Heavy Foot	Protected	Average	Drilled	–	Offensive Spearmen	8	4–6	0–6
Spanish mercenaries	Medium Foot	Protected	Average	Undrilled	–	Impact Foot, Swordsmen	7	6–8	0–8
Ligurian or Sikel mercenaries	Medium Foot	Protected	Average	Undrilled	–	Light Spear	5	6–8	0–8
Bolt-shooters — Only from 399	Heavy Artillery	–	Average	Drilled	Heavy Artillery	–	20	2	0–4
Special Campaigns									
Only Agathokles in Africa from 310 to 207									
Rowers etc. disguised as hoplites	Heavy Foot	Unprotected	Poor	Undrilled	–	–	2	6–8	0–12
Kyrenean allies									
Libyan allies – Late Libyan									
Numidian allies – Numidian or Early Moorish – See Field of Glory Companion 1: *Rise of Rome: Republican Rome at War*									
No Campanians, Ligurians, Sikels, Spanish or bolt-shooters permitted.									

SYRACUSAN ALLIES

Allied commander				Field Commander/Troop Commander			40/25	1	
Troop name	Troop Type				Capabilities		Points per base	Bases per BG	Total bases
	Type	Armour	Quality	Training	Shooting	Close Combat			
Greek cavalry	Cavalry	Armoured	Superior	Drilled	—	Light Spear, Swordsmen	17	4	0–4
			Average				13		
Campanian cavalry	Cavalry	Armoured	Superior	Drilled	—	Light Spear, Swordsmen	17	4	
Citizen hoplites	Heavy Foot	Protected	Average	Undrilled	—	Offensive Spearmen	7	6–8	0–8
			Average	Drilled			8		
			Poor	Undrilled			5		
			Poor	Drilled			6		
Mercenary hoplites	Heavy Foot	Protected	Average	Drilled	—	Offensive Spearmen	8	6–8	6–12
Archers	Light foot	Unprotected	Average	Undrilled or Drilled	Bow	—	5	4–6	0–6
Slingers	Light foot	Unprotected	Average	Undrilled or Drilled	Sling	—	4	4–6	0–6	0–12
Javelinmen	Light Foot	Unprotected	Average	Undrilled	Javelins	Light Spear	4	4–6	0–6
			Poor				2		
Gallic mercenaries	Heavy Foot	Protected	Average	Undrilled	—	Impact Foot, Swordsmen	7	4–6	0–6
Samnite or similar Italian mercenaries	Medium Foot	Protected	Average	Drilled	—	Light Spear, Swordsmen	7	4–6	0–6	0–12
Spanish mercenaries	Medium Foot	Protected	Average	Undrilled	—	Impact Foot, Swordsmen	7	4–6	0–6

ALEXANDRIAN MACEDONIAN

This list covers the armies of Alexander the Great and his father Philip, from 355 BC until the death of Alexander in 323 BC.

ALEXANDER THE GREAT

Born in 356 BC, Alexander was the son of King Philip II of Macedon. After an education that included the tutelage of Aristotle, Alexander assisted his father at the battle of Chaironeia in 338 BC, against an alliance of Greek city states led by Athens and Thebes, leading a decisive cavalry charge into the flank of the elite Theban Sacred Band. Macedonian control over Greece was thus assured and the Macedonians could turn their eyes towards their long-term goal of conquering the Persian Empire. In 336 BC, Philip

was assassinated, so it was left to Alexander, aged 20 and now King Alexander III of Macedon, to carry forward the great project.

In 334 BC, leaving Antipater as regent in Macedon, Alexander invaded Asia Minor with an army of 43,000 foot and 5–6,000 cavalry. He met and defeated the local Persian forces at the battle of Granikos. By 333 BC he had advanced to Syria, where he defeated the Persian Great King, Darius III, at Issos. After securing the Mediterranean coast and Egypt, he advanced into Mesopotamia, where he once again defeated Darius at Gaugamela in 331 BC. Darius fled and was murdered by one of his satraps. Alexander continued his eastwards advance. By 326 BC he had reached India,

Alexander's Foot Companions. Taken from *Men-at-Arms* 148: The Army of Alexander the Great.

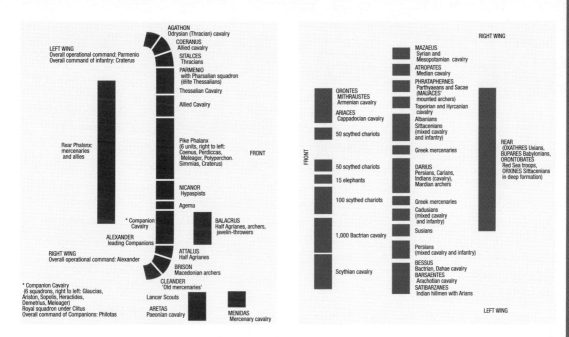

The battle of Gaugamela: Alexander's (red) and Darius' (blue) Order of Battle and Battle Stations
© Osprey Publishing Ltd. Taken from Campaign 7: Alexander the Great.

where he defeated the army of the local king Porus at the battle of Hydaspes. His army, exhausted by eight years of continuous marching and warfare, and frightened by tales of the huge numbers of elephants in the armies of the interior of India, refused to go further. Alexander was forced to turn back.

In 323 BC, in Babylon, at the age of 33, he died – how, no-one is certain. It was probably of illness but poisoning is a possibility. He had already conquered the eastern half of the "known world". Had he survived, he might well have gone on to conquer Carthage and Italy. His corpse was hardly cold before his generals started to fight over his empire. Thus began the Wars of the Successors and the break up of Alexander's mighty empire.

THE MACEDONIAN PHALANX

The Macedonian phalanx was developed by Philip II of Macedon and used by his son Alexander to conquer the Persian Empire. It continued to be dominant in Hellenistic warfare until the various successor kingdoms were conquered by the Romans and Parthians – see Field of Glory Companion 1: Rise of Rome: Republican Rome at War.

Hypaspists

The primary weapon of the phalanx was the sarissa, a pike approximately 5.5 metres (18 feet) in length, wielded with two hands. A shield smaller than the traditional hoplite aspis was strapped to the left arm. In addition, a helmet, greaves and linen body armour (thorax) were usually worn, and a short sword carried as secondary weaponry.

After Philip's reign, the pike phalanx was usually deployed 16 ranks deep, though on occasion this was halved to 8 ranks or doubled to 32. Five ranks of sarissa points projected beyond the front rank man, forming an impenetrable barrier as long as the phalanx remained in formation.

The Macedonian phalanx was a marked improvement on the hoplite phalanx and rendered it obsolete.

The Macedonian Companion cavalry were also innovative. Unlike earlier Greek cavalry these were shock troops, armed with the xyston, a 3.6m (12 ft) lance. They were used to deliver a decisive charge against a weak point in the enemy line.

Under Philip and Alexander the phalanx was mainly used to pin the enemy, while the Companion cavalry dealt the decisive blow. In the battles of Alexander's successors, which were mostly against other Macedonian style armies, the phalanx was used as the main arm of decision. When the Hellenistic kingdoms came into conflict with Rome, it became apparent that the rigid phalanx could not cope with the flexibility of the Roman legions.

TROOP NOTES

We allow for the various theories regarding the equipment of the Hypaspists. We also allow for the theory that most Greek mercenaries used by Alexander were Iphikratean hoplites.

ALEXANDRIAN MACEDONIAN STARTER ARMY		
Commander-in-Chief	1	Inspired Commander (Alexander)
Sub-commanders	2	2 x Troop Commander
Agema	1 BG	4 bases of Agema: Elite, Armoured, Drilled Cavalry – Lancers, Swordsmen
Thessalian heavy cavalry	1 BG	4 bases of Thessalian heavy cavalry: Superior, Armoured, Drilled Cavalry – Light Spear, Swordsmen
Thracian light horse	1 BG	4 bases of light horse: Average, Unprotected, Undrilled Light Horse – Javelins, Light Spear
Hypaspists	1 BG	6 bases of Hypaspists: Superior, Protected, Drilled Heavy Foot – Offensive Spearmen
Foot Companions	2 BGs	Each comprising 8 bases of Foot Companions: Average, Protected, Drilled Heavy Foot – Pikemen
Greek mercenary Iphikratean hoplites	1 BG	8 bases of Iphikratean hoplites: Average, Protected, Drilled Medium Foot – Offensive Spearmen
Agrianian javelinmen	1 BG	6 bases of javelinmen: Superior, Unprotected, Undrilled Light Foot – Javelins, Light Spear
Rhodian slingers	1 BG	6 bases of slingers: Average, Unprotected, Drilled Light Foot - Sling
Camp	1	Unfortified camp
Total	9 BGs	Camp, 12 mounted bases, 42 foot bases, 3 commanders

BUILDING A CUSTOMISED LIST USING OUR ARMY POINTS

Choose an army based on the maxima and minima in the list below. The following special instructions apply to this army:

- Commanders should be depicted as Agema or Companions.
- If the C-in-C is Alexander he must be an Inspired Commander.
- The minimum marked * applies if Philip or Alexander is present.
- Hypaspists must all be classified the same.
- Foot companions and hypaspists listed in a player's army list as heavy foot pikemen can instead be deployed at the start of the battle as medium foot with javelins – as in the army list below. A battle group of 12 heavy foot bases becomes two battle groups of 6 medium foot bases, a battle group of 8 heavy foot bases becomes a battle group of 8 medium foot bases. This option can only be used if they have been paid for at the points cost of the medium foot.

- Options only permitted from 328 BC or later cannot be used with more than 6 bases of Greek mercenary or allied traditional hoplites.

Thessalian Cavalry

Macedonian Pezhetairoi in training, by Christa Hook. Taken from *Warrior* 103: Macedonian Warrior.

ALEXANDRIAN MACEDONIAN

Territory Types: Agricultural, Developed, Hilly

C-in-C		Inspired Commander/Field Commander/Troop Commander					80/50/35		1	
Sub-commanders		Field Commander					50		0–2	
		Troop Commander					35		0–3	

Troop name		Troop Type				Capabilities		Points per base	Bases per BG	Total bases	
		Type	Armour	Quality	Training	Shooting	Close Combat				
Core Troops											
Agema		Cavalry	Armoured	Elite	Drilled	–	Lancers, Swordsmen	20	4	0–4	
Other Companion cavalry		Cavalry	Armoured	Superior	Drilled	–	Lancers, Swordsmen	17	4–6	4–6	4–12
Thessalian or Greek heavy cavalry		Cavalry	Armoured	Superior	Drilled	–	Light spear, Swordsmen	17	4–6	0–8	
				Average				13			
Prodromoi		Light Horse	Unprotected	Average	Drilled	–	Lancers, Swordsmen	8	4	0–4	
Thracian, Paionian or eastern light horse		Light Horse	Unprotected	Average	Undrilled	Javelins	Light Spear	7	4–6	4–6	
Hypaspists	Only before 328	Heavy Foot	Protected	Superior	Drilled	–	Offensive spearmen	10	6–8	*6–12	
		Medium Foot	Protected	Superior	Drilled	–	Offensive spearmen	10	6–8		
	Any date	Heavy Foot	Protected	Superior	Drilled	–	Pikemen	8	8–12		
Foot companions		Heavy Foot	Protected	Average	Drilled	–	Pikemen	6	8–12	12–36	
Agrianian javelinmen		Light Foot	Unprotected	Superior	Undrilled	Javelins	Light Spear	5	6–8	6–8	
Illyrian or Thracian javelinmen		Light Foot	Unprotected	Average	Undrilled	Javelins	Light Spear	4	6–8		
Cretan archers		Light Foot	Unprotected	Superior	Drilled	Bow	–	6	4–6	0–6	0–8
Macedonian archers		Light Foot	Unprotected	Average	Drilled	Bow	–	5	4–6	0–6	
Rhodian slingers		Light Foot	Unprotected	Average	Drilled	Sling	–	4	4–6	0–6	
Optional Troops											
Skythian horse archers	Only from 328	Light Horse or Cavalry	Unprotected	Average	Undrilled	Bow	Swordsmen	10	4–6		
Sogdian horse archers	Only from 328	Light Horse	Unprotected	Average	Undrilled	Bow	–	8	4–6	0–6	
Bactrian horse archers	Only from 328	Light Horse	Unprotected	Average	Undrilled	Bow	Light Spear	9	4–6		
Regrade hypaspists fighting with javelins instead of pike to:		Medium Foot	Protected	Superior	Drilled	–	Light Spear, Swordsmen	9	6–8	0–12	
Regrade foot companions fighting with javelins instead of pike to:		Medium Foot	Protected	Average	Drilled	–	Light Spear, Swordsmen	7	6–8	0–16	
Greek mercenary or allied traditional hoplites		Heavy Foot	Protected	Average	Drilled		Offensive Spearmen	8	6–8	0–36	
				Average	Undrilled			7			
				Poor	Undrilled			5			
Greek mercenary Iphikratean hoplites		Medium Foot	Protected	Average	Drilled		Offensive Spearmen	8	6–8		
Thracian peltasts		Medium Foot	Protected	Average	Undrilled		Light Spear	5	6–8	0–18	
		Medium Foot	Protected	Average	Undrilled		Offensive spearmen	7	6–8		
		Medium Foot	Protected	Average	Undrilled		Light Spear, Swordsmen	6	6–8		
		Medium Foot	Protected	Average	Undrilled		Heavy weapon	7	6–8		
Elephants	Only from 326	Elephants	–	Average	Undrilled			25	2	0–4	
Indian foot	Only in India from 326 to 325	Medium Foot	Unprotected	Average	Undrilled	Bow	Swordsmen	6	6–8	0–12	
				Poor				4			
Bolt-shooters or stone-throwers		Heavy artillery	–	Average	Drilled	Heavy Artillery	–	20	2	0–2	
Fortified camp								24		0–1	

EARLY SUCCESSOR

This list covers the armies of the Successors of Alexander from his death in 323 BC until the advent of Rome. It covers both the early wars for supremacy amongst the Successors, and the later more stable phase when the bulk of Alexander's empire was divided into the three kingdoms of Macedon, Egypt and the Seleucid kingdom in the East.

The armies of Pyrrhos of Epeiros from 280 BC, the Antigonid kingdom of Macedon from c.260 BC, the Seleucid kingdom from 205 BC, and the Ptolemaic kingdom of Egypt from 166 BC, are covered by separate lists in Field of Glory Companion 1: *Rise of Rome: Republican Rome at War*.

Antigonos Monophthalmos ("One-Eye") was based in Asia Minor. He was defeated and killed in 301 BC, but his grandson, Antigonos Gonatas ("Knock-Knees"), made himself King of Macedon in 277 BC. Lysimachos was based in Thrace. He was defeated and killed in 281 BC.

Xystophoroi

EARLY SUCCESSOR (LYSIMACHID) STARTER ARMY		
Commander-in-Chief	1	Field Commander (Lysimachos)
Sub-commanders	2	2 x Troop Commander
Xystophoroi	1 BG	4 bases of xystophoroi: Superior, Armoured, Drilled Cavalry – Lancers, Swordsmen
Thracian heavy cavalry	1 BG	4 bases of Thracian heavy cavalry: Superior, Armoured, Undrilled Cavalry – Light Spear, Swordsmen
Thracian light horse	1 BG	4 bases of light horse: Average, Unprotected, Undrilled Light Horse – Javelins, Light Spear
Phalangites	2 BGs	Each comprising 8 bases of phalangites: Average, Protected, Drilled Heavy Foot – Pikemen
Greek hoplites	2 BGs	Each comprising 6 bases of hoplites: Average, Protected, Undrilled Heavy Foot – Offensive Spearmen
Thracian foot	2 BGs	Each comprising 6 bases of Thracian foot: Average, Protected, Undrilled Medium Foot – Heavy Weapon
Archers	1 BG	6 bases of archers: Average, Unprotected, Undrilled Light Foot – Bow
Slingers	1 BG	6 bases of slingers: Average, Unprotected, Undrilled Light Foot - Sling
Camp	1	Unfortified camp
Total	11 BGs	Camp, 12 mounted bases, 52 foot bases, 3 commanders

BUILDING A CUSTOMISED LIST USING OUR ARMY POINTS

Choose an army based on the maxima and minima in the list below. The following special instructions apply to this army:

• Commanders should be depicted as xystophoroi or phalangites.

• The minima marked * do not apply if the C-in-C is Antigonos Gonatas and he has Galatian allies.

• Thureophoroi and thorakitai can be graded as Medium Foot or Heavy Foot, but all of both types must be graded the same.

EARLY SUCCESSOR

Territory Types: Agricultural, Developed, Hilly

C-in-C	Inspired Commander/Field Commander/Troop Commander					80/50/35		1	
Sub-commanders	Field Commander					50		0–2	
	Troop Commander					35		0–3	

Troop name		Troop Type				Capabilities		Points per base	Bases per BG	Total bases
		Type	Armour	Quality	Training	Shooting	Close Combat			
Core Troops										
Xystophoroi		Cavalry	Armoured	Superior	Drilled	–	Lancers, Swordsmen	17	4–6	*4–12
				Average				13		
Thracian, Persian or other irregular heavy cavalry		Cavalry	Armoured	Superior	Undrilled	–	Light spear, Swordsmen	16	4–6	0–6
				Average				12		4–12
Greek or Thessalian heavy cavalry		Cavalry	Armoured	Superior	Drilled	–	Light spear, Swordsmen	17	4–6	
				Average				13		
Elite phalangites		Heavy Foot	Protected	Superior	Drilled	–	Pikemen	8	8–12	0–12
Other phalangites		Heavy Foot	Protected	Average	Drilled	–	Pikemen	6	8–12	*12–48
Greek mercenary Iphikratean hoplites	Only before 279	Medium Foot	Protected	Average	Drilled		Offensive Spearmen	8	6–8	Seleucids, Ptolemies or Lysimachos 0–8, Others 6–24
Greek mercenary thureophoroi	Only from 279	All Medium Foot or all Heavy Foot	Protected	Average	Drilled	–	Offensive Spearmen	8	6–8	
Javelinmen		Light Foot	Unprotected	Average	Drilled or Undrilled	Javelins	Light Spear	4	6–8	0–12
Archers		Light Foot	Unprotected	Average	Drilled or Undrilled	Bow	–	5	6–8	0–12	6–24
Slingers		Light Foot	Unprotected	Average	Drilled or Undrilled	Sling	–	4	6–8	0–12
Optional Troops										
Light cavalry		Light Horse	Unprotected	Average	Undrilled or Drilled	Javelins	Light Spear	7	4–6	0–8
Skythian horse archers	Only Seleucids	Light Horse or Cavalry	Unprotected	Average	Undrilled	Bow	Swordsmen	10	4	0–4
Mede, Parthian or similar horse archers	Only Antigonos One–Eye or Seleucids	Light Horse	Unprotected	Average	Undrilled	Bow	–	8	4	
Greek hoplites	Only Lysimachos or Macedon	Heavy Foot	Protected	Average	Undrilled	–	Offensive Spearmen	7	6–8	0–16
					Drilled			8		
Egyptian phalangites	Only Ptolemies from 217	Heavy Foot	Protected	Poor	Drilled	–	Pikemen	4	8–12	0–24
Thracians, Kappadokians, Lykians, Mysians, Pamphylians or similar		Medium Foot	Protected	Average	Undrilled	–	Light Spear	5	6–8	Lysimachos 12–24, Others 0–8
Thracians	Only before 250	Medium Foot	Protected	Average	Undrilled	–	Offensive Spearmen	7	6–8	
	Only before 300	Medium Foot	Protected	Average	Undrilled	–	Light Spear, Swordsmen	6	6–8	
	Any date	Medium Foot	Protected	Average	Undrilled	–	Heavy weapon	7	6–8	
Illyrians	Only Lysimachos	Medium Foot	Protected	Average	Undrilled	–	Offensive Spearmen	7	6–8	0–8
Cretans		Light Foot	Unprotected	Superior	Drilled	Bow	–	6	6–8	0–8
Upgrade thureophoroi to thorakitai	Only Seleucids or Macedon from 279	Medium Foot or Heavy Foot	Armoured	Average	Drilled	–	Offensive Spearmen	10	6–8	0–8
Galatians	Only from 279	Heavy Foot	Protected	Superior	Undrilled	–	Impact Foot, Swordsmen	9	6–8	0–8
				Average				7		

Elephants	Lysimachos or Ptolemies before 279	Elephants	–	Average	Undrilled	–	–	25	?	0–2
	Seleucids before 279									0–6
	Seleucids or Ptolemies from 279 or others at any date									0–4
Scythed chariots	Only Seleucids	Scythed Chariots	–	Average	Undrilled	–	–	15	2–4	0–4
Arab camelry	Only Seleucids or Ptolemies	Camelry	Unprotected	Poor	Undrilled	Bow	Swordsmen	10	4	0–4
Low quality garrison troops	Only Ptolemies	Medium Foot	Protected	Poor	Drilled	–	Light Spear	4	6–8	0–8
Massed levies	Only Seleucids	Mob	Unprotected	Poor	Undrilled	–	–	2	6–8	0–8
Bolt–shooters or stone–throwers	Heavy artillery	–	Average	Drilled	Heavy Artillery	–	20	2	0–2
Fortified camp								24		0–1
Allies										
Galatian mercenary allies (Only Macedon from 277 – Antigonos Gonatas).										
Special Campaigns										
Only Lysimachos and Seleukos at Ipsos in 301										
Use the higher of the two leaders' minima and maxima.										

EARLY SARMATIAN

This list covers the armies of the Sarmatian tribes from the mid-4th century BC until the 1st century AD. At the greatest extent of their territory they ruled from the Volga to the Danube.

TROOP NOTES

The main strength of Sarmatian armies was their horsemen. Iazygian and Siracae cavalry were mostly lancers by this period, carrying but not making much military use of bows. Scale armour for man and horse was popular, sometimes metal, mainly of horn or lacquered leather. Many Siracae lancers were unarmoured. The Rhoxolani were slow to adopt the lance, most of their cavalry retaining an older style of equipment comprising bow, light spear, wicker shield and leather armour. Some Sarmatian women fought as warriors, wearing the same costume as the men, but with long braided hair. Sarmatian armies could also include a fair number of subject foot. The Siracae early on gave up the nomadic life, settling in hill forts from which they ruled a subject population of agricultural peasants, fielding 20,000 horse and 22,000 foot in 310 BC.

EARLY RHOXOLANI STARTER ARMY

Commander-in-Chief	1	Field Commander
Sub-commanders	2	2 x Troop Commander
Lancers	2 BGs	Each comprising 4 bases of lancers: Superior, Armoured, Undrilled Cavalry – Lancers, Swordsmen
Other cavalry	4 BGs	Each comprising 4 bases of other cavalry: Superior, Protected, Undrilled Cavalry – Bow*, Light Spear, Swordsmen
Scouts	1 BG	4 bases of scouts: Average, Unprotected, Undrilled Light Horse – Bow, Swordsmen
Foot archers	2 BGs	Each comprising 6 bases of foot archers: Average, Unprotected, Undrilled Light Foot – Bow
Foot javelinmen	1 BG	6 bases of foot javelinmen: Average, Unprotected, Undrilled Light Foot – Javelins, Light Spear
Camp	1	Unfortified camp
Total	10 BGs	Camp, 28 mounted bases, 18 foot bases, 3 commanders

BUILDING A CUSTOMISED LIST USING OUR ARMY POINTS

Choose an army based on the maxima and minima in the list below. The following special instructions apply to this army:

- Commanders should be depicted as lancers.
- An army must either be of the Siracae, the Iazyges or the Rhoxolani. Only options belonging to one tribe can be used.
- Minima marked * apply if any non-allied foot are used.

EARLY SARMATIAN

Territory Types: Steppes, Agricultural

Troop name		Troop Type				Capabilities		Points per base	Bases per BG	Total bases
		Type	Armour	Quality	Training	Shooting	Close Combat			
C-in-C		Inspired Commander/Field Commander/Troop Commander						80/50/35		1
Sub-commanders		Field Commander						50	0–2	
		Troop Commander						35	0–3	
Core Troops										
Lancers	Only Siracae or Iazyges	Cavalry	Armoured	Superior	Undrilled	–	Lancers, Swordsmen	16	4–6	16–54
			Protected					12		
	Only Rhoxolani	Cavalry	Armoured	Superior	Undrilled	–	Lancers, Swordsmen	16	4–6	0–16
Other cavalry	Only Rhoxolani	Cavalry	Protected	Superior	Undrilled	Bow*	Light Spear, Swordsmen	14	4–6	16–40
Scouts		Light Horse	Unprotected	Average	Undrilled	Bow	Swordsmen	10	4–6	0–8
Foot archers		Light Foot	Unprotected	Average	Undrilled	Bow	–	5	6–8	*12–24
				Poor				3		
		Medium Foot	Unprotected	Average	Undrilled	Bow	–	5	6–8	
				Poor				3		
Foot javelinmen		Medium Foot	Protected	Average	Undrilled		Light Spear	5	6–8	*6–24
				Poor				3		
		Light Foot	Unprotected	Average	Undrilled	Javelins	Light Spear	4	6–8	
				Poor				2		
Optional Troops										
Slingers		Light Foot	Unprotected	Average	Undrilled	Sling	–	4	4–6	0–6
				Poor				2		
Poor quality foot		Mob	Unprotected	Poor	Undrilled	–	–	2	8–12	0–12
Allies										
Skythian allies – Later Skythian or Saka – See Field of Glory Companion 1: Rise of Rome: Republican Rome at War.										

EARLY SARMATIAN ALLIES

Allied commander	Field Commander/Troop Commander						40/25		1	
Troop name		Troop Type				Capabilities		Points per base	Bases per BG	Total bases
		Type	Armour	Quality	Training	Shooting	Close Combat			
Lancers	Only Siracae or Iazyges	Cavalry	Armoured	Superior	Undrilled	–	Lancers, Swordsmen	16	4–6	4–16
			Protected					12		
	Only Rhoxolani	Cavalry	Armoured	Superior	Undrilled	–	Lancers, Swordsmen	16	4–6	0–4
Other cavalry	Only Rhoxolani	Cavalry	Protected	Superior	Undrilled	Bow*	Light Spear, Swordsmen	14	4–6	4–12
Foot archers		Light Foot	Unprotected	Average	Undrilled	Bow	–	5	6–8	0–8
				Poor				3		
		Medium Foot	Unprotected	Average	Undrilled	Bow	–	5	6–8	
				Poor				3		
Foot javelinmen		Medium Foot	Protected	Average	Undrilled	–	Light Spear	5	6–8	0–8
				Poor				3		
		Light Foot	Unprotected	Average	Undrilled	Javelins	Light Spear	4	6–8	
				Poor				2		

GALATIAN

The Galatians were a group of Celtic tribes who invaded Macedonia, Greece and Thrace in 280 BC. They were eventually ousted by Antigonos Gonatas. Three tribes, the Trocmi, Tolistobogii and Tectosages crossed over to Asia Minor at the invitation of Nicomedes I of Bithynia, who wanted their help against his brother. They proceeded to devastate Asia Minor. They were eventually defeated by the Seleucid king Antiochos I at the "Elephant Victory" in 273 BC in which their cavalry, chariots and scythed chariots were panicked by the Seleucid elephants. Following this they settled in central Anatolia, this region subsequently being known as Galatia. They supported themselves by raiding and by hiring themselves out as mercenaries.

In 189 BC they were defeated by the Romans under Gnaeus Manlius Vulso. Thereafter their power declined. During the reign of Mithridates VI of Pontus, they came under Pontic hegemony. In 64 BC, following the defeat of Mithridates, Galatia became a Roman client state under the chieftains (tetrarchs) of the three tribes. The tetrarch of the Tolistobogii, Deiotarus, was soon

after raised by the Romans to the status of king. He re-organised his army as Roman style legionaries – raising two full legions. After suffering heavy losses in the defeat of Domitius by Pharnaces of Pontus, the survivors were regrouped into one legion, and took part in Caesar's victory over Pharnaces at Zela in 47 BC. When Galatia was annexed as a Roman province in 25 BC, these troops became the Legio XXII Deiotariana. They were posted to Egypt where they were stationed at Alexandria. The legion was probably destroyed by the Jews during the revolt of Simon Bar Kokhba (132–135 BC).

This list covers Galatian armies from their invasion of Greece until Galatia was incorporated as a a Roman province.

Galatian Chariot

GALATIAN STARTER ARMY

Commander-in-Chief	1	Field Commander
Sub-commanders	2	2 x Troop Commander
Chariots	1 BG	4 bases of chariots: Superior, Undrilled Light Chariots – Light Spear
Cavalry	2 BGs	Each comprising 4 bases of cavalry: Superior, Protected, Undrilled Cavalry – Light Spear, Swordsmen
Warriors	4 BGs	Each comprising 8 bases of warriors: Superior, Protected, Undrilled Heavy Foot – Impact Foot, Swordsmen
Javelinmen	1 BG	8 bases of javelinmen: Average, Unprotected, Undrilled Light Foot – Javelins, Light Spear
Camp	1	Unfortified camp
Total	8 BGs	Camp, 12 mounted bases, 40 foot bases, 3 commanders

BUILDING A CUSTOMISED LIST USING OUR ARMY POINTS

Choose an army based on the maxima and minima in the list below. The following special instructions apply to this army:

- Commanders should be depicted as cavalry or chariots.
- All warriors must be of the same quality grade.

GALATIAN

Territory Types: Agricultural, Hilly, Mountains

C-in-C		Inspired Commander/Field Commander/Troop Commander					80/50/35	1	
Sub-commanders		Field Commander					50	0–2	
		Troop Commander					35	0–3	

Troop name		Troop Type				Capabilities		Points per base	Bases per BG	Total bases
		Type	Armour	Quality	Training	Shooting	Close Combat			
Core Troops										
Chariots	Only before 62	Light Chariots	–	Superior	Undrilled	–	Light Spear	15	4–6	0–6
Cavalry		Cavalry	Armoured	Superior	Undrilled	–	Light Spear, Swordsmen	16	4–6	0–6 / 4–24
		Cavalry	Protected	Superior	Undrilled	–	Light Spear, Swordsmen	12	4–6	4–24
Warriors	Only before 62	Heavy Foot	Protected	Superior	Undrilled	–	Impact Foot, Swordsmen	9	8–12	18–120
	Only from 227	Heavy Foot	Protected	Average	Undrilled	–	Impact Foot, Swordsmen	7	8–12	
Imitation legionaries	Only from 62	Heavy Foot	Protected	Average	Drilled	–	Impact Foot, Swordsmen	8	4–8	0–48
Optional Troops										
Javelinmen		Light Foot	Unprotected	Average	Undrilled	Javelins	Light Spear	4	6–8	0–8
Fortified camp								24		0–1
Special Campaigns										
Only from 280 to 279										
Greek foot		Medium Foot or Heavy Foot	Protected	Average	Drilled	–	Offensive Spearmen	8	4–6	0–6
Paionians		Light Foot	Unprotected	Average	Undrilled	Javelins	Light Spear	4	6–8	0–12
		Medium Foot	Protected	Average	Undrilled	–	Light Spear	5	6–8	
Only in 273										
Scythed chariots		Scythed Chariots	–	Average	Undrilled	–	–	15	2–4	0–4
Only in 189										
Paphlagonians & Kappadokians		Medium Foot	Protected	Average	Undrilled	–	Light Spear	5	6–8	0–8

GALATIAN ALLIES

Allied commander		Field Commander / Troop Commander						40/25		1		
Troop name		**Troop Type**				**Capabilities**		Points per base	Bases per BG	Total bases		
		Type	Armour	Quality	Training	Shooting	Close Combat					
Cavalry		Cavalry	Armoured	Superior	Undrilled	–	Light Spear, Swordsmen	16	4	0–4	0–8	
		Cavalry	Protected	Superior	Undrilled	–	Light Spear, Swordsmen	12	4–6	0–8		
Warriors	Only before 62	Heavy Foot	Protected	Superior	Undrilled	–	Impact Foot, Swordsmen	9	8–12	0–32	12–32	
	Only from 227	Heavy Foot	Protected	Average	Undrilled	–	Impact Foot, Swordsmen	7	8–12			
Imitation legionaries	Only from 62	Heavy Foot	Protected	Average	Drilled	–	Impact Foot, Swordsmen	8	4–8	0–18		

HELLENISTIC GREEK

This list covers mainland Greek armies from 279 BC until Greece was incorporated as a Roman province in 146 BC.

TROOP NOTES

During this period, some hoplites were replaced by thureophoroi and some by pikemen.

Thureophoroi carried a large oval shield (thureos), probably copied from the Galatians, and usually wore a helmet but no body armour or greaves. They thus appear to have been a development of the Iphikratean hoplite. When fighting in the main battle line, they used a long thrusting spear, with a sword as secondary weapon. Sometimes they operated as euzonoi, substituting their spears for javelins and deploying as skirmishers. Some thureophoroi wore chain mail body armour and were called thorakitai.

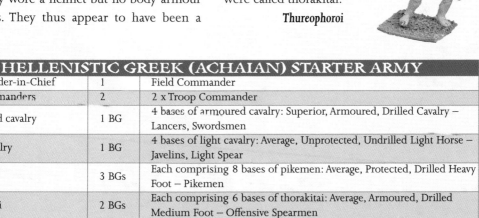

Thureophoroi

HELLENISTIC GREEK (ACHAIAN) STARTER ARMY

Commander-in-Chief	1	Field Commander
Sub-commanders	2	2 x Troop Commander
Armoured cavalry	1 BG	4 bases of armoured cavalry: Superior, Armoured, Drilled Cavalry – Lancers, Swordsmen
Light cavalry	1 BG	4 bases of light cavalry: Average, Unprotected, Undrilled Light Horse – Javelins, Light Spear
Pikemen	3 BGs	Each comprising 8 bases of pikemen: Average, Protected, Drilled Heavy Foot – Pikemen
Thorakitai	2 BGs	Each comprising 6 bases of thorakitai: Average, Armoured, Drilled Medium Foot – Offensive Spearmen
Thureophoroi	2 BGs	Each comprising 6 bases of thureophoroi: Average, Protected, Drilled Medium Foot – Offensive Spearmen
Slingers	1 BG	6 bases of slingers: Average, Unprotected, Undrilled Light Foot - Sling
Camp	1	Unfortified camp
Total	10 BGs	Camp, 8 mounted bases, 54 foot bases, 3 commanders

BUILDING A CUSTOMISED LIST USING OUR ARMY POINTS

Choose an army based on the maxima and minima in the list below. The following special instructions apply to this army:

- Commanders should be depicted as light horse if Aitolian, otherwise as cavalry.
- Minima marked * apply only if C-in-C is of that origin.
- Whether Athens or Elis continued to field hoplites is uncertain. The minimum marked ** therefore only applies if the C-in-C is Boiotian.
- Unless the C-in-C is of the same origin, troops only permitted to a certain origin

can only be fielded under the command of an allied general of that origin. An allied general's contingent must conform to the Hellenistic Greek allies list below, but the troops in the contingent are deducted from the minima and maxima in the main list.

- Spartans from 227 BC to 222 BC cannot have more than 24 pikemen.
- Thureophoroi and thorakitai can be graded as Medium Foot or Heavy Foot, but all of both types must be graded the same.

Aitolian Javelinman

Commander Amompharetos and his men at the battle of Plataea, 479 BC, by Richard Hook. Taken from Elite 66: The Spartan Army.

HELLENISTIC GREEK

Territory Types: Agricultural, Developed, Hilly, Mountains									
C-in-C	Inspired Commander/Field Commander/Troop Commander						80/50/35	1	
Sub-commanders	Field Commander/Troop Commander						50/35	0–2	
Greek allied commanders	Field Commander/Troop Commander						40/25	0–3	
Troop name		Troop Type			Capabilities		Points per base	Bases per BG	Total bases
		Type	Armour	Quality	Training	Shooting	Close Combat		

Troop name		Type	Armour	Quality	Training	Shooting	Close Combat	Points per base	Bases per BG	Total bases
Core Troops										
Armoured cavalry	Any	Cavalry	Armoured	Average	Drilled	–	Light Spear, Swordsmen	13	4–6	4–6
					Undrilled			12		
	Only Achaians from 208 or Athenians	Cavalry	Armoured	Superior	Drilled	–	Lancers, Swordsmen	17	4–6	
				Average				13		
Light cavalry		Light Horse	Unprotected	Average	Undrilled or Drilled	Javelins	Light Spear	7	4–6	0–6
Thureophoroi		All Medium Foot or all Heavy Foot	Protected	Average	Drilled	–	Offensive spearmen	8	6–8	8–108
Hoplites	Only Boiotians before 270, Athenians or Eleians	Heavy Foot	Protected	Average	Undrilled	–	Offensive Spearmen	7	6–8	**16–48
					Drilled			8		
	Only Spartans before 227	Heavy Foot	Protected	Superior	Drilled	–	Offensive Spearmen	10	6–8	*6–16
	Only Spartans before 221	Heavy Foot	Protected	Average	Drilled	–	Offensive Spearmen	8	6–8	*8–32
Pikemen	Only Boiotians from 245, Achaians from 208 or Spartans from 227	Heavy Foot	Protected	Average	Drilled	–	Pikemen	6	8–12	*16–48
Javelinmen	Only Aitolians	Light Foot	Unprotected	Average	Undrilled	Javelins	Light Spear	4	6–8	*24–120
	Others									0–12
Euzonoi		Light Foot	Protected	Average	Drilled	Javelins	Light Spear	5	6–8	0–12
Archers		Light Foot	Unprotected	Average	Undrilled or Drilled	Bow	–	5	6–8	0–8
Slingers		Light Foot	Unprotected	Average	Undrilled	Sling	–	4	6–8	0–8
Optional Troops										
Thorakitai	Only Achaians	All Medium Foot or all Heavy Foot	Armoured	Average	Drilled	–	Offensive spearmen	10	6–8	0–12
Illyrians	Only Achaians	Medium Foot	Protected	Average	Undrilled	–	Offensive Spearmen	7	4–6	0–12
Bolt–shooters		Heavy Artillery		Average	Drilled	Heavy Artillery	–	20	2	0–2
Special Campaigns										
Only Eleians in 207										
Roman allies – Mid Republican Roman – See Field of Glory Companion 1: Rise of Rome: *Republican Rome at War*.										
Only Achaians in 146										
Freed slaves		Heavy Foot	Protected	Poor	Drilled	–	Pikemen	4	8–12	0–24

The Archers total bases note "6–12" appears to the right of the Archers/Slingers rows.

HELLENISTIC GREEK ALLIES

Allied commander		Field Commander/Troop Commander					40/25	1	
Troop name		**Troop Type**				**Capabilities**	**Points per base**	**Bases per BG**	**Total bases**
		Type	Armour	Quality	Training	Shooting	Close Combat			

Troop name		Type	Armour	Quality	Training	Shooting	Close Combat	Points per base	Bases per BG	Total bases
Armoured cavalry	Any	Cavalry	Armoured	Average	Drilled	–	Light Spear, Swordsmen	13	4	0–4
					Undrilled			12		
	Only Achaians from 208 or Athenians	Cavalry	Armoured	Superior	Drilled	–	Lancers, Swordsmen	17	4	
				Average				13		
Light cavalry		Light Horse	Unprotected	Average	Undrilled or Drilled	Javelins	Light Spear	7	4	0–4
Thureophoroi		All Medium Foot or all Heavy Foot	Protected	Average	Drilled	–	Offensive spearmen	8	6–8	6–24
Hoplites	Only Boiotians before 270, Athenians or Eleians	Heavy Foot	Protected	Average	Undrilled	–	Offensive Spearmen	7	6–8	**6–16
					Drilled			8		
	Only Spartans before 227	Heavy Foot	Protected	Superior	Drilled	–	Offensive Spearmen	10	6–8	0–6
	Only Spartans before 221	Heavy Foot	Protected	Average	Drilled	–	Offensive Spearmen	8	6–8	*6–12
Pikemen	Only Boiotians from 245, Achaians from 208 or Spartans from 227	Heavy Foot	Protected	Average	Drilled	–	Pikemen	6	8–12	*8–16
Javelinmen	Only Aitolians	Light Foot	Unprotected	Average	Undrilled	Javelins	Light Spear	4	6–8	*6–24
	Others									0–8
Archers		Light Foot	Unprotected	Average	Undrilled or Drilled	Bow	–	5	4	0–4
Slingers		Light Foot	Unprotected	Average	Undrilled	Sling	–	4	4	

Hoplites in battle, by Steve Noon. Taken from Campaign 188: Thermopylae 480 BC.

GRAECO-BACTRIAN

The Graeco-Bactrian Kingdom was founded circa 250 BC when Diodotos, the Seleucid governor of Bactria, Sogdiana and Margiana, seizing his opportunity while King Antiochos II was otherwise occupied with a war against Ptolemaic Egypt, declared his territory independent. At its greatest extent, the kingdom covered modern Uzbekistan, Turkmenistan, Tajikistan, Afghanistan and parts of Iran and Pakistan.

C.210 BC, Bactria was invaded by the Seleucid King Antiochos III. This war, however, ended in a negotiated peace, in which Antiochos recognised King Euthydemos.

C.180 BC, Demetrios, son of Euthydemos, invaded India, which was in some disarray following the fall of the Mauryan Empire. By 175 BC the Indo-Greek kingdom had been established. Soon after this, the overthrow of the Eythydemid dynasty in Bactria led to the Bactrian and Indian sections of the kingdom splitting apart.

The Parthian conquest of the eastern provinces of the Seleucid kingdom, under Mithridates I (170–138 BC) cut the Graeco-Bactrian and Indo-Greek kingdoms off from direct contact with the west.

Following this, the territories of the Bactrian kingdom were eroded by the nomadic Yue-chi and the last Graeco-Bactrian king, Heliokles, abandoned Bactria and retreated to his Indian holdings c. 130 BC.

This list covers the armies of the Graeco-Bactrian kingdom from the revolt of Diodotos until the fall of the kingdom to the Yue-chi.

GRAECO-BACTRIAN STARTER ARMY		
Commander-in-Chief	1	Field Commander
Sub-commanders	2	2 x Troop Commander
Iranian lancers	2 BGs	Each comprising 4 bases of Iranian lancers: Superior, Heavily Armoured, Undrilled Cataphracts – Lancers, Swordsmen
Bactrian light cavalry	2 BGs	Each comprising 4 bases of Bactrian light cavalry: Average, Unprotected, Undrilled Light Horse – Bow, Light Spear
Saka cavalry	1 BG	4 bases of Saka cavalry: Average, Unprotected, Undrilled Light Horse – Bow, Swordsmen
Phalanx	2 BGs	Each comprising 8 bases of pikemen: Average, Protected, Drilled Heavy Foot – Pikemen
Thureophoroi	1 BG	6 bases of thureophoroi: Average, Protected, Drilled Medium Foot – Offensive Spearmen
Mountain Indian archers	1 BG	6 bases of Mountain Indian archers: Average, Unprotected, Undrilled Light Foot - Bow
Elephants	1 BG	2 bases of elephants: Average, Undrilled Elephants
Camp	1	Unfortified camp
Total	10 BGs	Camp, 22 mounted bases, 28 foot bases, 3 commanders

BUILDING A CUSTOMISED LIST USING OUR ARMY POINTS

Choose an army based on the maxima and minima in the list below. The following special instructions apply to this army:

- Commanders should be depicted as Greek lancers.
- The minimum marked * only applies if any foot are used.

GRAECO-BACTRIAN

Territory Types: Agricultural, Steppe

Troop name		Troop Type				Capabilities		Points per base	Bases per BG	Total bases
C-in-C		Inspired Commander/Field Commander/Troop Commander						80/50/35	1	
Sub-commanders		Field Commander						50	0–2	
		Troop Commander						35	0–3	
		Type	Armour	Quality	Training	Shooting	Close Combat			
Core Troops										
Greek lancers		Cavalry	Armoured	Superior	Drilled	–	Lancers, Swordsmen	17	4–6	0–6
				Average				13		
Iranian lancers	Any date	Cavalry	Armoured	Superior	Undrilled	–	Lancers, Swordsmen	16	4–6	6–18
				Superior	Drilled			17		
				Average	Undrilled			12		
				Average	Drilled			13		
	Only from 210	Cataphracts	Heavily Armoured	Superior	Undrilled	–	Lancers, Swordsmen	18	4–6	
				Superior	Drilled			20		
				Average	Undrilled			14		
				Average	Drilled			16		
Bactrian light cavalry		Light Horse	Unprotected	Average	Undrilled	Bow	Light Spear	9	4–6	6–18
Phalanx		Heavy Foot	Protected	Average	Drilled	–	Pikemen	6	8–12	*8–24
Thureophoroi		Medium Foot or Heavy Foot	Protected	Average	Drilled	–	Offensive spearmen	8	6–8	0–8
Euzonoi		Light Foot	Protected	Average	Drilled	Javelins	Light Spear	5	6–8	
Elephants		Elephants	–	Average	Undrilled	–	–	25	2	0–4
Optional Troops										
Saka cavalry		Light Horse or Cavalry	Unprotected	Average	Undrilled	Bow	Swordsmen	10	4–6	0–6
Mountain Indian cavalry		Light Horse	Unprotected	Average	Undrilled	Javelins	Light Spear	7	4–6	0–6
Mountain Indian spearmen		Medium Foot	Protected	Average	Undrilled	–	Light Spear	5	6–8	0–16
Mountain Indian archers		Light Foot	Unprotected	Average	Undrilled	Bow	–	5	6–8	0–16
		Medium Foot	Unprotected	Average	Undrilled	Bow	–	5		
Cretans		Light Foot	Unprotected	Superior	Drilled	Bow	–	6	4–6	0–6
Fortified camp								24		0–1
Allies										
Saka allies – Later Skythian or Saka – See Field of Glory Companion 1: Rise of Rome: *Republican Rome at War*.										

INDO-GREEK

Circa 180 BC, The Graeco-Bactrian King Demetrios invaded India, which was in some disarray following the fall of the Mauryan Empire. By 175 BC, the Indo-Greek kingdom had been established. Soon after this, the Eythydemid dynasty in Bactria was overthrown, which led to the Bactrian and Indian sections of the kingdom splitting apart.

Under King Menander I, who ruled from circa 155 to 130 BC, the Indo-Greek kingdom was greatly expanded, covering much of north-west and northern India.

Indian Archer

Thereafter, there were at least two separate Indo-Greek kingdoms, in the east and west of the Greek-ruled territories. The Yue-chi took over most of the western kingdom c.70 BC.

The last Indo-Greek king, Strato II, ruled in the eastern Punjab until he was overthrown by the Indo-Skythians c.10 AD.

This list covers the armies of the Greek kingdoms in India from the invasion of India by Demetrios, until the fall of the last kingdom.

TROOP NOTES

Classification of the Greek cavalry is based on coins of Hermaios showing Greek cavalrymen armed with bow and spear. We assume that they were not specialist horse archers.

INDO-GREEK STARTER ARMY		
Commander-in-Chief	1	Field Commander
Sub-commanders	2	2 x Troop Commander
Greek cavalry	1 BG	4 bases of Greek cavalry: Superior, Armoured, Drilled Cavalry – Bow*, Light Spear, Swordsmen
Indian cavalry	1 BG	4 bases of Indian cavalry: Average, Unprotected, Undrilled Cavalry – Light Spear
Saka cavalry	1 BG	4 bases of Saka cavalry: Average, Unprotected, Undrilled Light Horse – Bow, Swordsmen
Phalanx	2 BGs	Each comprising 8 bases of pikemen: Average, Protected, Drilled Heavy Foot – Pikemen
Thureophoroi	1 BG	6 bases of thureophoroi: Average, Protected, Drilled Medium Foot – Offensive Spearmen
Indian archers	2 BGs	Each comprising 8 bases of Indian archers: Average, Unprotected, Undrilled Medium Foot – Bow, Swordsmen
Elephants	2 BGs	Each comprising 2 bases of elephants: Average, Undrilled Elephants
Camp	1	Unfortified camp
Total	10 BGs	Camp, 16 mounted bases, 38 foot bases, 3 commanders

BUILDING A CUSTOMISED LIST USING OUR ARMY POINTS

Choose an army based on the maxima and minima in the list below. The following special instructions apply to this army:

- Commanders should be depicted as Greek cavalry.

INDO—GREEK

Territory Types: Agricultural, Hilly, Woodlands, Tropical

C-in-C	Inspired Commander/Field Commander/Troop Commander					80/50/35	1	
Sub-commanders	Field Commander					50	0–2	
	Troop Commander					35	0–3	

Troop name	Troop Type				Capabilities		Points per base	Bases per BG	Total bases
	Type	Armour	Quality	Training	Shooting	Close Combat			
Core Troops									
Greek cavalry	Cavalry	Armoured	Superior	Drilled	Bow*	Light Spear, Swordsmen	19	4–6	0–6
			Average				15		
Indian cavalry	Cavalry	Unprotected	Average	Undrilled	–	Light Spear	6	4–6	4–6
		Unprotected	Poor				4		
		Protected	Average				7		
		Protected	Poor				5		
Phalanx	Heavy Foot	Protected	Average	Drilled	–	Pikemen	6	8–12	8–16
Thureophoroi	Medium Foot or Heavy Foot	Protected	Average	Drilled	–	Offensive spearmen	8	6–8	0–8
Euzonoi	Light Foot	Protected	Average	Drilled	Javelins	Light Spear	5	6–8	
Indian archers	Medium Foot	Unprotected	Average	Undrilled	Bow	Swordsmen	6	6–8	8–60
			Poor				4		
Indian javelinmen	Medium Foot	Protected	Average	Undrilled	–	Light Spear, Swordsmen	6	6–8	0–16
			Poor				4		
Elephants	Elephants	–	Average	Undrilled	–	–	25	2	0–4
Optional Troops									
Saka cavalry	Light Horse or Cavalry	Unprotected	Average	Undrilled	Bow	Swordsmen	10	4–6	0–6
Mountain Indian cavalry	Light Horse	Unprotected	Average	Undrilled	Javelins	Light Spear	7	4–6	0–6
Mountain Indian spearmen	Medium Foot	Protected	Average	Undrilled	–	Light Spear	5	6–8	0–16
Mountain Indian archers	Light Foot	Unprotected	Average	Undrilled	Bow	–	5	6–8	0–16
	Medium Foot	Unprotected	Average	Undrilled	Bow	–	5		
Cretans	Light Foot	Unprotected	Superior	Drilled	Bow	–	6	4–6	0–6
Fortified camp							24		0–1
Allies									

Indian allies – Classical Indian

Saka allies – Later Skythian or Saka – See Field of Glory Companion 1: Rise of Rome: *Republican Rome at War.*

APPENDIX 1 – USING THE LISTS

To give balanced games, armies can be selected using the points system. The more effective the troops, the more each base costs in points. The maximum points for an army will usually be set at between 600 and 800 points for a singles game for 2 to 4 hours play. We recommend 800 points for 15mm singles tournament games (650 points for 25mm) and 1000 points for 15mm doubles games.

The army lists specify which troops can be used in a particular army. No other troops can be used. The number of bases of each type in the army must conform to the specified minima and maxima. Troops that have restrictions on when they can be used cannot be used with troops with a conflicting restriction. For example, troops that can only be used "before 450 BC" cannot be used with troops that can only be used "from 450 BC". All special instructions applying to an army list must be adhered to. They also apply to allied contingents supplied by the army.

All armies must have a C-in-C and at least one other commander. No army can have more than 4 commanders in total, including C-in-C, sub-commanders and allied commanders.

All armies must have a supply camp. This is free unless fortified. A fortified camp can only be used if specified in the army list. Field fortifications and portable defences can only be used if specified in the army list.

Allied contingents can only be used if specified in the army list. Most allied contingents have their own allied contingent list, to which they must conform unless the main army's list specifies otherwise.

BATTLE GROUPS

All troops are organized into battle groups. Commanders, supply camps and field fortifications are not troops and are not assigned to battle groups. Portable defences are not troops, but are assigned to specific battle groups.

Battle groups must obey the following restrictions:

- The number of bases in a battle group must correspond to the range specified in the army list.
- Each battle group must initially comprise an even number of bases. The only exception to this rule is that battle groups whose army list specifies them as 2/3 of one type and 1/3 of another, can comprise 9 bases if this is within the battle group size range specified by the list.
- A battle group can only include troops from one line in a list, unless the list specifies a mixed formation by specifying fractions of the battle group to be of types from two lines. e.g. 2/3 spearmen, 1/3 archers.
- All troops in a battle group must be of the same quality and training. When a choice of quality or training is given in a list, this allows battle groups to differ from each other. It does not permit variety within a battle group.
- Unless specifically stated otherwise in an army list, all troops in a battle group must be of the same armour class. When a choice of armour class is given in a list, this allows battle groups to differ from each other. It does not permit variety within a battle group.

EXAMPLE LIST

Here is a section of an actual army list, which will help us to explain the basics and some special features. The list specifies the following items for each historical type included in the army:

- Troop Type – comprising Type, Armour, Quality and Training.

- Capabilities – comprising Shooting and Close Combat capabilities.
- Points cost per base.
- Minimum and maximum number of bases in each battle group.
- Minimum and maximum number of bases in the army.

Troop name		Troop Type				Capabilities		Points per base	Bases per BG	Total bases
		Type	Armour	Quality	Training	Shooting	Close Combat			
Xystophoroi	Only before 274 BC	Cavalry	Armoured	Superior	Drilled	–	Lancers, Swordsmen	18	4–6	4–6
Javelin-armed heavy cavalry	Before 274 BC	Cavalry	Armoured	Superior	Drilled	–	Light Spear, Swordsmen	17	4–6	4–6
				Average				14		
	From 274 BC	Cavalry	Armoured	Superior	Drilled	–	Light Spear, Swordsmen	17	4–6	6–12
				Average				14		
Hoplites		Heavy Foot	Protected	Average	Drilled	–	Offensive Spearmen	8	6–8	0–18
		Heavy Foot	Protected	Average	Undrilled	–	Offensive Spearmen	7		
				Poor				5		
Archers		Light Foot	Unprotected	Average	Drilled	Bow	–	5	6–8	0–12
Slingers		Light Foot	Unprotected	Average	Drilled	Sling	–	4	6–8	0–12
Javelinmen		Light Foot	Unprotected	Average	Undrilled	Javelins	Light Spear	4	6–8	0–12

(6–18 spanning Archers/Slingers/Javelinmen Total bases)

SPECIAL FEATURES:

- Xystophoroi can only be used before 274 BC. Javelin-armed heavy cavalry can be used before or after 274 BC but the minimum and maximum numbers permitted change. Thus before 274 BC, the army can and must include from 4 to 6 bases of xystophoroi and from 4 to 6 bases of javelin-armed heavy cavalry. From 274 BC the army cannot include any bases of xystophoroi but can and must include from 6 to 12 bases of javelin-armed heavy cavalry.
- Javelin-armed heavy cavalry can either be Superior or Average. The list specifies the different points costs. All the bases in a battle

group must be of the same quality.
- Hoplites can be Average Drilled, Average Undrilled or Poor Undrilled. All the bases in a battle group must be of the same quality and training. The total number of hoplite bases in the army cannot exceed 18.
- The army is allowed from 0 to 12 bases each of archers, slingers and javelinmen. However, the total number of archers, slingers and javelinmen bases must be at least 6 and cannot exceed 18. Each battle group must have from 6 to 8 bases of one type – a battle group cannot include a mixture of archers and slingers or javelinmen.

APPENDIX 2 – THEMED TOURNAMENTS

A tournament based on the "Immortal Fire" theme can include any of the armies listed in this book.

It can also include the following armies from our other army list books. These can only use options permitted between 550 BC and 146 BC:

Field of Glory Companion 1: *Rise of Rome: Republican Rome at War.*

Pyrrhic

Illyrian

INDEX